VOICES

Messages from pop artists, jazz musicians, blues and C&W singers – those who have used their voices to bring pleasure to the world

Dorothy Davies

VOICES

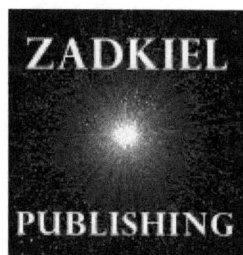

ZADKIEL

PUBLISHING

This book is divided into four sections, namely:-

Pop Mania
Country Roads
Colour Me Blues
Jazz Inc

SECTION 1 - POP MANIA

A COLLECTION OF REMINISCENCES BY POP ARTISTS

With the help of Brian Jones and Gene Pitney

POP MANIA

Grateful thanks:

To **Brian Jones** and **Gene Pitney** for their help in bringing the people to me so they could speak about their lives, deaths and afterlives.

To Mary Holliday for her invaluable input in this extraordinary book

To Terry Wakelin, still the rock and anchor in my life;

To my spirit companions for laughter and more love than a human could ask for.

Most of all, to the many artists who took time out from their spirit lives to come and talk.

A small admission here, one that occurred to me just about the time I was thinking of wrapping this book up. Back when I was a pre- and very young teenager, I sent a letter to a teen magazine to ask whether any of the stars on the enclosed list would come to my birthday party. I had a charming note back saying they would be too busy to come.

It's time to say... thinking about it, all the names on my list have now come to see me, now they have time (and so do I) to talk with them. Wishes can come true, you just need to believe...

The artists who have left messages in the order they arrived: (The titles are the songs they chose for their message heading.

2006:
Freddie Mercury - *Bohemian Rhapsody*

2007:
Brian Jones - *Ruby Tuesday*
Dusty Springfield - *Son Of A Preacher Man*

2008:
John Lennon - *Imagine*
Del Shannon - *Runaway*
Billy Fury - *Wondrous Place*
Gene Pitney - *Something's Got A Hold Of My Heart*
Lonnie Donegan - *Rock Island Line*
Rick Nelson - *Hello Marylou*
Eddie Cochran - *Summertime Blues*
Alma Cogan - *Hernando's Hideaway*
Marc Bolan - *Ride A White Swan*
Bob Marley - *No Woman No Cry*
Jim Morrison - *Riders On The Storm*
Buddy Holly - *That'll Be The Day*
George Harrison - *My Sweet Lord*
Jimi Hendrix - *Purple Haze*
Lawrence Payton (Four Tops) - *Yesterday's Dreams*
Otis Redding - *(Sitting On) The Dock Of The Bay*
Ray Charles - *Georgia On My Mind*
Guy Mitchell - *Singing The Blues*
Roy Orbison - *Only The Lonely*
Sam Cooke - *You Send Me*
Bobby Darin - *Dream Lover*
Bo Diddley - *Bo Diddley*
Cass Elliot - *Monday, Monday*
Johnny Ray - *Just Walking In The Rain*
Marvin Gaye - *I Heard It Through The Grapevine*

Ike Turner - *River Deep, Mountain High*
Frankie Laine - *I Believe*
David Whitfield - *Answer Me*
Frankie Vaughan - *Green Door*
Big Bopper - *Chantilly Lace*

2009:
Perry Como - *Catch A Falling Star*
Anthony Newley - *I've Waited So Long*
Carl Perkins - *Blue Suede Shoes*
Ritchie Valens - *La Bamba*

2010:
Harry Chapin - *W O L D*
Mel Appleby - *Respectable*
Karl Mueller - *Runaway Train*
Flanders and Swan - *The Hippopotamus Song*
Nat 'King' Cole - *Unforgettable*
Janis Joplin - *Piece Of My Heart*
Kirsty McColl - *Walking Down Madison*
Dean Martin - *Memories Are Made Of This*
Alan Breeze - *I've Got a Lovely Bunch Of Coconuts*
Michael Hutchence - *Need You Tonight*
Marie Lloyd - *The Boy I Love Is Up In The Gallery*
Floyd Cramer - *On The Rebound*
Ian Dury - *Reasons To Be Cheerful, Part 3*

2011:
Gerry Rafferty - *Baker Street*
Kurt Cobain - *Smells Like Teen Spirit*
John Walker - *No Regrets*
Phyllis Hyman - *Never Say Never Again*

2012:
Richard Manuel - *The Night They Drove Old Dixie Down*
Whitney Houston - *I Will Always Love You*

Donna Summer - *I Feel Love*
Robin Gibb -*Massachusetts*
Shannon Hoon- *No Rain*

2013:
Max Bygraves *Tulips From Amsterdam*

2017:
Amy Winehouse *Rehab*
Levi Stubbs *– Look Of Love*
Vesta Victoria *– Waiting At the Church*

2018:
Chuck Berry *– Maybelline*
Michael Jackson - *Thriller*

2006

Bohemian Rhapsody

Freddie Mercury

5th September 1946 – 24th November 1991

In 2006 I bought tickets for a Queen Tribute evening for my friend Mary and myself.

The next time I visited Mary, she pulled a video from the shelf and said, "Let's watch the real thing, shall we?"

As we were watching Freddie parading across the stage, every inch the showman, we became aware of someone standing behind the sofa where we were sitting. I asked who it was and got "guess." We tried our usual Twenty Questions but the person got impatient and said right in my ear, "you're looking at him!" I jumped so hard it hurt!

He watched for a while and then said "show-off, wasn't I?" and I said "No, showman, not show off." He seemed pleased with that.

Freddie came and went for a while; then I heard from a medium that he had taken on the task of helping young musicians and singers who were making their demo tapes, work he could and does do very well.

I still get visits from this charismatic beautiful man; he drops by to see if I am all right, to exchange a few words and then he is gone again, back to his first love, working with music.

There has not been a direct message from Freddie. I know well that he resented his early passing, he hated the disease which took him, he wished for much more time on this side of life and a chance to do all the things

13

he really wanted to do. It seemed to him he was cut down in his prime although he accepts it was his time to go. He appreciates the fact that the music lives on, he smiles at the 'tribute' bands and hopes they keep Queen music alive but, as he says, they will never replace the real thing.

2007

Ruby Tuesday

Brian Jones

28th February 1942 – 3rd July 1969

I am writing this in October 2007, a date which indicates that Brian Jones, the golden Stone, has been with me on and off for the past eight years. It feels as if he has been here forever. His gentle presence is always welcome and he is always loved.

It took me some time to realise that Brian was actually with me, not just channelling thoughts to me through Alan J. Miles, a talented medium who is a great fan of Brian. Constant references by mediums to 'do you know a Brian?' finally got through to me, especially when one friend finally said, with impatience, 'it's Brian Jones!' I kept asking the question why, why me, my usual perpetual persistent question. No answer, none at all. Just an insistence that he was there. At that time I was in touch with a composer/musician and Brian indicated he would like to go and work with him. I know my friend saw Brian for a fleeting moment; I also know he has helped a good deal with various musical problems and even some chords. I thought all was well and was glad I could be a bridge from one to the other.

Then, in the summer of 2007, that same medium friend was giving a trance demonstration at our monthly meeting. His Cockney guide came through and immediately came to me to say, "You know Brian Jones, don't you, Missus?" I said yes, I did. He said "He's all right but he's better when he's with you, Missus," and so Brian came back to be part of my team.

I know there is no such thing as coincidence; the Rolling Stones were headlining the Isle of Wight Festival that night. After a long talk in the car going home, when Brian and I discussed various aspects of his life and needs, he said he wanted to go and see the Stones, saying he had not been to see them since he'd passed over. He went, but I had the feeling it was not a good idea. It wasn't, he came back distraught; having to admit for the first time it really was all over. They had changed, he had changed but in a different way and he had no connection with them anymore. It was the beginning of the rehabilitation process for Brian. Those who go to spirit with unresolved issues need to face up to them, find a way of working out a solution to the guilt, regret, forgiveness needed or to be given or whatever else it is that is bothering them.

Brian spent a lot of time with my shaman, Snow, discussing spiritual matters. I used to see them and sensed them when they were together; it was a lovely feeling. Snow moved on in 2008 to take a seat on the spirit Council which supervises all that we do. Another great Native American came to take his place. Brian has been consulting with him… the spiritual discussions go on and my team remains as full as ever.

August 2010

I had a 'Brian says' right there but Brian has decided not to give his thoughts like that. In common with some of the others, he is leaving it to me to write his page.

Brian is a gentle presence, a golden presence, when he comes. He spends a good deal of his time in meditation and reflection, still recovering from his experiences in his former life. Some souls take longer than others to recover, because some are more badly damaged than others.

Of his death he says nothing, of his life he says it was good and he would have liked longer to be part of the Rolling Stones, in part for the adulation it brought, in part for the joy of making music – even if it was slated by the critics for the longest time, He smiles at the thought.

His input to **Voices** is incalculable. I would not be building this book without his help.

He asks that people remember him. I would say he would be very difficult to forget.

Son Of A Preacher Man

Dusty Springfield

16th April 1939 – 2nd March 1999

Dusty came lightly into my life in 2007, stayed for a
month or so and then quietly disappeared again. I felt she
came to check me out, to see if I was right for the job. It
seems I was, as among the others are now coming, she
has let me know she is there. I admired her very much
when she was at the peak of her career and still like the
lilting yet powerful tones she brings to her singing. She
is a delicate spirit, very beautiful in every way.

September 2008.

At my desk, knowing someone told me to open the file
Voices, quietly waiting to see who wishes to come and
speak tonight. I heard the whisper 'Dusty' and am filled
with the presence of the lovely lady who went too soon.
I am aware of a gentle scent and a gentle presence.

Dusty says:

I loved my time as a performer, loved the spotlight, the
limelight if you like. Loved the attention even though we
all know, those of us who are in that spotlight, that it can
end in a moment or it can last forever. Those like
Sinatra, Elvis, the great ones, will go on forever. The rest
of us do carry a small fear, even in the Realms, that we
will be forgotten. I know this is why Alma has come, a
name that surprised our dear channel but also pleased
her, as we all seem to have done.

A small diversion: I want to say how wonderful it is
to be accepted. Few mediums will do that; they will say

18

it is their imagination and dismiss the person. This dear channel does not; her first reaction is always 'welcome, thank you for coming.' I have heard her say it many times, regardless of who the person is, whether she actually liked their music or not. Overall I would say she did and she does, for there is little that she does not listen to.

But that is not why I am here, she is reminding me, I am here to talk about my life in spirit and my feelings about my passing. I was deeply sad to go home. I had been performing for a good many years, got used to being a star, got used to adulation and luxury and then the invasive crippling cancer began its work and literally gobbled me up. I had time to mourn the passing of a career, to be aware of what it was doing to me, how it was making me look, someone who had taken great pride in their appearance. I hated the cancer with a deadly hatred as much for the way it made me look as for what it was doing to me.

My passing was quiet; I slipped gently into the Realms. Once there I began to wonder why I had been so angry, so full of hatred. I had a period of hospitalisation to put everything right, including removing my anger and hate and then I realised how much I had been given, what freedom I had to go where I wanted, visit who I wanted, even if they did not know I was there. I could drop in on this friend or family member, make sure they were happy, tweak a little thing of their life here and there if I could to encourage that happiness, or try some upliftment if they were down.

I also realised I could work with new upcoming girl singers, so if anyone says someone sounds like or works like Dusty Springfield, that will be my influence creeping in. I am glad to be able to help, to work, to guide by nudges and pushes any promising young singers, because I know how tough the industry is and how savage critics and fans can be. You need all the help you can get.

This is my chance and I wish to take it to say thank you to all my fans over the years, thank you for all the support, the encouragement, the applause and the love you gave me. It was tremendous. If I decide to come back and live another lifetime on this earth plane, I would hope I could find someone to like a lot, to give them my money by buying their music and attending their concerts, just as you all did for me.

Thanks for allowing me to be part of **Voices**, to be immortalised in this way means I will never be forgotten. For that I am eternally grateful.

2008

Imagine

John Lennon

9ᵗʰ October 1940 – 8ᵗʰ December 1980

May 2008.

A medium writes to me, someone called John, with brown hair and lots of energy, has come through as she is tuning in to draw a portrait for me. Do I know who it is? Answer, at that moment, no, I don't. But my friend Mary immediately said 'John Lennon' when I told her. This is the second time he has made himself known to me. This time it is more serious, I accept he is here and wanting to work with me. The portrait was not of John Lennon, but another John, a family member I did not know. I am still awaiting John Lennon's arrival. I know he will come, in his own time.

John says:

It's been a long time since I decided I wanted to be part of this project – a long time in your terms but here there is no time, so it was a bit of a surprise to see how long it had actually been. Over two years in fact, it's August 2010.

Well, what can you say about the phenomenon that was the Beatles? We hoped for fame, who doesn't when they start out? We all think we sound the best/look the best/write the best stuff but more times than not we don't, which is why so many fall by the wayside, never get further than playing in the local club, pub or cafe. But we took off, and how!

Fame does strange things to you. It gives you a sense of omnipotence, so when we got all mystical and strange, it seemed odd to us that others didn't like it, that they thought we were the strange ones, while we thought what we were doing was perfectly natural. The love affair with the public and the public with us changed perceptibly over that; reinforced for a while with Sergeant Pepper, which I see is still regarded as a classic, but then fell away again.

The break up was inevitable, I feel. Sad for our fans, but right for us. Disputes over this and that created rifts that could not be properly healed over. It was time to go our separate ways and then I got to do the music I really wanted to do, that I had always wanted to do but which didn't fit the Beatles. Seriously, can you imagine the Beatles doing Imagine? I don't think so.

It all ended so abruptly. There and not there, one lunatic with a gun, one life over. I've noticed that some of the others who have been to talk have said they weren't sorry. I was. I wanted to do more, record more, write more, spend a good many years with Yoko and it didn't happen. It obviously wasn't meant to happen but that doesn't stop me being disappointed.

Some time has gone by now and I've got used to the idea that my life was cut short, that there would be no further albums and good times on your side of life. I live through Julian's music to a certain degree and for that I am grateful. I am sad that George passed over when he did; he had much to offer still. Paul, well, what can I say to my old mate who seemed to lose his way with a certain wife, except hope he finds some happiness with someone before it's his turn to pack it all in.

I am glad to be in this book, in truth I would have hated to be left out!

Runaway

Del Shannon

30th December 1934 – 8th February 1990

June 2008

In the middle of listening to a Gene Pitney track, Del Shannon suddenly came to mind. Again, this does not happen 'normally' but the overwhelming feeling was that Del was there and that was confirmed when I went to ebay to buy a CD of his greatest hits. The YES feeling I got was so strong I all but fell off my chair.

Del Shannon is straight out of my teen years, a charismatic, charming singer. I am glad he is here.

July 2011 –I have reached Del's page and asked him to come.

Del says:

Is it that long since I approached you? Sorry! Been so busy looking up all my friends and having a really good time... truthfully, a much better time than I had during many of my years on your side of life. I have to ask, what comes first, the alcohol or the depression? And how many who have come to you suffered from the twin evils? Your newest arrival did, I know that. I haven't met up with him yet but I will.

The good times were good. The bad times were so bad I couldn't carry on. Simple as that. Sorry, sorry, sorry to all my fans, it was not good for you and certainly not good for my family but oh, I couldn't face another day.

Now each day is a bright new one filled with happiness, with spirit work – I work with those who suffered from the twin evils in your life – and everything is wonderful. I want to say thank you for calling me to finish this page. I've been meaning to come, I promise you!

Wondrous Place

Billy Fury

17th April 1940 – 28th January 1983

It's the 19th June 2008.

On the way to work this morning I was listening to Gene Pitney when a line in one of his songs reminded me of a Billy Fury song. Instantly I became aware of Billy around me. He was extremely emotional and I drove with eyes full of tears, spirit tears, because he didn't expect me to recognise him immediately and accept him as immediately as I did. He thought he would have to send me songs, as others had, to make me aware of him. No, he's someone I loved dearly during my teen years; all his records are still loved by me. And so, for fifteen minutes or so I drove, full of emotion and happiness, that this treasured person has come to be part of the book. I am very honoured and happy he has come.

Billy says:

if I had worked less and taken more care, I could have gone on a bit longer, perhaps, but in truth, I had done all I wanted to do in the music world. That last album was a sop to my ego more than anything, for the real work was with the birds and animals, the caring for the farm, the working with and living with Nature. It's the most dreadful cliché but in my case it happened to be true. I'm not sorry it ended when it did, for I was tired, my body had said clearly it had done enough, thank you. I knew that any night would be my last; that I would simply not wake up. I knew it that night when I went to bed I knew I would wake in another world.

This world is finer than I ever thought possible. Here are many animals to take care of, not that they need it, but it is something we human spirits can do, take care of the animals and birds and they respond with all the love they used to give us on your side of life. I am content that my name lives on, my music lives on; my fame is big enough still to attract people to my work, my songs, my statue, which pleases me very much. You tend to think that when you pass on that is the end, you are forgotten, buried in the vaults of outdated music. It is very good for me to know that is not so. I grieve for my brother's unhappiness and wish there was a way I could let him know I'm fine and well and singing when I want and taking care of a whole menagerie of animals and birds, which is pleasing me every day that I am here.

Albie, my dear brother, ease your heart and mind. Your brother Ronnie is fine.

Something's Got A Hold Of My Heart

Gene Pitney

17ᵗʰ February 1940 – 5ᵗʰ April 2006

'Something's Got A Hold Of My Heart' had been in my head for several days and I kept asking, as I do when there is a persistent song, who is around me. No answer, but the song persisted. It suddenly changed to "The Man Who Shot Liberty Valance" which took all doubts away. Only Gene Pitney would give me that song! Mary said; when I spoke to her about him, that he had come to be the main editor of the book. The others, she said, would come and then go, but he would stay to oversee the whole thing. He often decides to throw a complete medley of his songs at me, tipping them one over the other, ending usually with "I'm Gonna Be Strong" his favourite out of all of them.

Gene is an outstanding performer/singer and earned all the accolades given to him over the years. He is very gentle in his vibration, very loving and friendly and a really good organiser. The book has come together with his help.

Gene says:

'I'm Gonna Be Strong' is my favourite of all my songs but I chose 'Something's Got A Hold Of My Heart' as my title as it is one of the most evocative ones, you could write endless stories from those lyrics - and it happens to be the favourite of my channel, so...

I've been a long time coming to give the world my message, too busy racing around tracking down people who want to be in the book but haven't come forward with their messages. Unfortunately for human beings, there is no time in spirit and so they tend to forget someone is here waiting patiently, year after year...

Life was good. Life was rich and wonderful, devoted fans, great musicians and recording engineers, first class studios to record in – I could go on but it isn't necessary. It was all good and it worked. I had a good life. I didn't expect it to be over quite so soon but – we can't choose how long we have, it is all part of the great plan that we go when our lives are done, by spirit standards, not ours. I am content with all I did, few could ask for more than I had.

So, I am taking the chance to say thank you to all the fans, all the musicians, song writers, everyone involved in my career, thanks for making it so wonderful.

Rock Island Line

Lonnie Donegan

29th April 1931 – 4th November 2002

July 1st 2008

Seriously spending time looking for a particular Lonnie Donegan CD… and wondering why…

Then I realised Lonnie was around, with that infectious smile and zest for life that epitomised all his music. He is someone from my teen years, someone I loved, laughed over and admired. Again, his coming to me is an honour. Impressions will come when he visits me properly. At the moment I am only aware of a presence and his laughter. My spirit companions found "Does Your Chewing Gum Lose Its Flavour" absolutely hysterical. I'm glad I am the only person who sees and hears them at times…

August update. Lonnie is often around, not to speak directly as the others have done. I am aware he wants to say he loved every moment of his career, the songs, the recording process, the live performances; all of it became one whole life which he lived and loved. He was sad when it ended but not that sad that he could not say 'it was wonderful.' He's happy to be recognised and accepted as a spirit person. He has not tried to make contact with many people, knowing how difficult it is for someone 'famous' to be accepted. He knows full well that "The Ballad of New Orleans" drives me mad, as once in my head it will not go. His favourite trick is to arrive, as it were, with 'Rock Island Line' and having got my attention, launch into that song and stand back, laughing, when I say things like 'Lonnie, I'll kill you!'

But it's done with love and the intention of making me laugh. He said today I haven't laughed much lately and he wants to cheer me up. He does that just by being there, as he is a delightful, loving, friendly presence.

April 2009

Lonnie sent me a message via a friend's circle recently, so I know he is still around and watching out for my wellbeing. He is a charming and loving man.

June 2017

Working on this book and mentioning that it is now a common occurrence for me to be aware of Lonnie's smiling vibrant presence, when he stops by to see if I am all right.

Hello Mary-Lou

Ricky Nelson

8th May 1940 - 31st December 1985

July 2008

People are turning up all over the place and at the oddest times, too. I was listening to the Travelling Wilburys in my car on my way home from work when I became aware of Rick Nelson around me. This was without his bringing me a song to indicate who he was. He grinned so much when I recognised him it was untrue and grinned even more when I told him his presence filled me with happiness.

That night I sat circle and had an intense and lovely meditation. I went to a thatched house where Rick was waiting.

December 2008

I stopped work on Henry VIII's book, knowing someone was around to give me a message but that someone waited until I'd scrolled through all the names and then I reached this one. Thank you, Rick… you could have said… the laughter is ringing in my ears.

Rick says:

A good life, a life of music. A life of exposure on TV and in the media in every way. TV was good for me, for a while, the singing was good for me for a long while but then, like many things, it went away and left me. But oh the heyday of my career, the 'Hello Marylou' days as I think of them, when I could seemingly do no wrong! It was wonderful, it was a dream come true, it was – everything.

Then everything went away. It left me with debts, with problems, with children and a failing marriage. It was so unbelievably sad, but I wanted to work on, to make more music, more films, more TV, more life, I guess. I wanted to give more love; that was a fact.

But the plane went down.

And did it ever go down!

I think most of us were dead when it burst into flames, I have to say that. I don't think any of us were burned; I would not like to think we were.

This channel is asking, was I sad it was over. In truth, no. I wanted more music, more films and more TV but knowing the fragility of the business, the fickleness of fans as well as producers and directors, it could not be guaranteed. In many ways, it was best it was over and done with.

I have my fame. My music lives on in countless ways. There are websites dedicated to me, I am in the Rock 'n' Roll Hall of Fame and now in this book… could there be better ways to be remembered? The most important thing to me is that the music lives on, for I lived for my music and I loved my music. Yes, it was pop, yes it was to some degree cheesy but it was good, it lifted people's spirits, they could dance to it, smooch to it, whatever. It was important, it is important.

In many ways this life is better. 'And you work…' I am being asked. Yes, I work with those who write songs which are 'pop' and make the charts and make people smile. No one could ask for more than that.

To be recognised, to be remembered, to be cared about, even on this side of life, it is an essential part of our well-being. It has given me the confidence to approach others now, to see if I can work even more with upcoming songsters and lyricists and to tell them who I am, rather than just be a presence.

Summertime Blues

Eddie Cochran

2nd October 1938 – 17th April 1960

11th July 2008

It's not usual to be given the name Eddie Cochran when about to fall off to sleep but it happened that night. Eddie is a welcome visitor and an essential part of this book.

Eddie's music is 'sunshine', from the era when all the songs were full of life, bounce, vitality and most of all, youth.

Eddie comes with that persona, full of lightness, full of energy still. His pleasure is in knowing that his songs live on, that there are websites dedicated to him, that his music is still heard, that even though his career was relatively short, he left us a lasting memory and a legacy of fine instantly recognisable music.

Eddie says:

Gene, Sharon and I were in this taxi. I remember how happy I was, my fiancé with me, my friend with me, we were playing well and singing well, Sharon and I were so in love it was untrue. Everything in my world was wonderful, career opening up unbelievably well, everyone loving the music, loving the band, loving me.

I've gotta say this, if you have to die, what better moment to do it than when the whole world loves you and your life is on its highest peak. I mean, it could have gone downhill, Sharon and I could have split, I could have fallen out with the record company – it happened to others – I'd already lost Buddy and Ritchie in the plane crash, friends die, family die, so… yes, it was sad. Yes, I

33

would have liked a lot more years. Yes, I mourned for Sharon and my family and friends; their grief was overwhelming and hard for me to come to terms with. But, every one of us has a time to go home. That was my time. I didn't understand the reasoning, I don't even now know what part my passing played in the great Master Plan that is the spirit world, but I do not argue with their logic or their decision. It had to be.

And, like I said, if you have to go, is there a finer moment than that peak, when you believe nothing could be better than this?

Since I've been in the spirit world I've worked with, coached silently and encouraged a lot of young men to learn to play the guitar properly, not go off half-cocked into the music world. It's not easy out there, the critics are damning, the fans fickle. You need to know what you're at, know your music, know your lyrics, pour your heart into all you do, knowing you only get the fame for a short time anyway, unless you happen to be a Rolling Stone or a Beatle or Bob Dylan, you know what I'm saying. But there are those with great talent, great ability and I draw near to them and coax them and push them as much as I can. Not one knows I am there.

Until you welcomed me to be part of this book, no one has truly recognised or spoken with me. Some have tried but they were people I didn't trust enough to draw close to. It's easy to be drawn into a trap of someone who is not purely and simply in the light. You send a beacon out, a bright white light and we draw close to it like moths, really like a bunch of moths. We know you don't mind.

Hernando's Hideaway

Alma Cogan

19th May 1932 – 26th October 1966

July 2008 –

If anything was guaranteed to ensure this book was not my imagination, the arrival of Alma Cogan was it. She was a remarkably lively young lady when she was in her prime, before the cancer took her, that is, and her vibration is gentle, bubbly and full of life. She gave me her name rather than one of her songs, which I would not have recognised. She said she does not want to be forgotten. I knew her name instantly, she will not be forgotten.

Alma says:

One of the biggest problems some of us in spirit have to cope with is the sense of being forgotten outside of family and friends. We had our moment of fame, our brief 'candle flame' if you like and when the candle went out, we are afraid no one will recall our songs, our lives, our time. In part this is what this book is about; some who are coming are in that category. Others are coming because it is a chance to express their feelings about their music and their lives and even more importantly, what they are doing in the spirit realms. So before I talk about my life and career, I want to say I encourage, help and guide where I can anyone who has or has passed through having ovarian cancer. It is a particularly nasty cancer which affects a woman's deepest being, that which provides the basis of life. When I can, I visit sufferers on your side of life to try and encourage them and when any cross over I am there to help with the counselling that we have when we go into the spirit world, if we have suffered such a debilitating and awful condition.

Back to fame and fortune. 'The girl with the giggle in her voice' that was me, ever trying not to laugh but knowing sometimes it bubbled up and came out in the music. I loved life to that degree, that everything was good, was fun, was joyous. Love for everyone in my life, too. The cancer came as a nasty shock and I went home at what was for many a very young age. I mourned the loss of my career and my family and friends for some time, until I realised I had been given a wonderful chance to really do something worthwhile and wonderful, to help people with the same cancer. I have been doing that ever since and for the foreseeable future, will go on doing it, too, until those that guide me here tell me I am ready to move on.

I give thanks for this chance to speak. It's been a pleasure and a delight. My fame is secured forever in your book. It has been and will continue to be a delight.

Ride A White Swan

Marc Bolan

30th September 1947 – 16th September 1977

11th July 2008

Whilst telling my friend Mary about the book, she said 'I also see Marc Bolan' and yes, he is very much there. T Rex was a powerhouse of a band and Marc was a powerhouse of a front man. Glam rock at its best.

Initial thoughts and impressions: Marc said he realised the car was going out of control but, contrary to common beliefs, his life did not flash before his eyes, even though he knew it was his time. What happened was, he stood outside the crushed car looking at his mangled body and then his life flashed before his eyes, the time with the band, the fickle public, the interest and then non-interest, those he had loved, those he had not loved. He recalls thinking it wasn't a bad way to go.

August 2008.

Marc is close tonight. I asked for his message for the book.

Marc says:

'Glam rock' is an odd name for a musical movement, but it sums it up perfectly in many ways. It was outrageous but it gave us a chance to play with colours, outfits, hairstyles, makeup and shoes and boots and let everyone think what they wanted about our sexuality, it was nothing to do with them anyway! It never seemed to occur to anyone we just liked dressing up … maybe we hadn't fully grown up, but then who cares? It fitted the time, the scene, the music.

I loved making music. I loved the pounding beat, the surge of energy, the powerhouse that was created by the band. I have used the word you used, I see that, but it describes T Rex perfectly. Even the 'quieter' tracks, like Ride A White Swan still had immense power behind them.

We were famous. We were T Rex. Everyone knew us, everyone had heard of us, many loved us. Was I sorry it ended? Yes, in some ways. Not in others. Everything has to end. I was glad it ended fast, not long drawn out suffering with some incurable disease, especially the one called old age. Truthfully, I see the photos in the magazines, I peer over people's shoulders sometimes, just to see what the aged rockers look like these days. I see them and I think, I died young, good-looking and full of life. I would rather have it end that way than be old, tired, photographed in before-and-after sections in the papers. They would have had a field day with me. I would have grown old disgracefully, I know that.

What have I done with myself since being on the other side? Helped a few groups here and there, dropped in on recording sessions and got the engineers to alter a few settings to make things sound better without them knowing why they did it but knowing they were pleased with the result. Spent time with young poets, helping them to write and giving them the confidence to stand up and read their work in public when they got the chance. Spent time with young actors making their first steps into the profession, giving them a confidence boost when they needed it most. Spreading myself about, yes, but nothing in particular, just going here and there, doing what I can where I can, never staying too long so anyone would work out that they were being 'helped'. I prefer it that way.

I am very, very grateful for this chance to say some words about the band, the music and what I do now. It is good to know T Rex is not forgotten, it is good to know there is a legacy of music out there.

Since I went home I have been able to help many people. I have been glad to do it. I could not have done it if I had lived.

I send my thanks to all who remember T Rex, to all who helped us be the huge success we were, to those who followed us and were T Rex fans, many thanks. I have not forgotten you. I am glad you have not forgotten me.

As to where my money went, that is something I know but –

That's all I'm going to say on that subject!

No Woman No Cry

Bob Marley

6ᵗʰ February 1945 – 11ᵗʰ May 1981

My friend Mary, when consulted about the shape of this book, said 'I see a page with Bob Marley's name on it'. At that time he had not contacted me. His music is not something I used to listen to, but I bought a CD and it proved to be a delight; it has so much resonance even now, many years after his passing. I await Mr Marley's visits with great anticipation.

I have played the CD several times now and came to the same conclusion each time; this is 'sunshine music' - with a message. The gentle rhythms and Bob Marley's outstanding voice create a magical mixture that no other reggae artist has ever achieved. Definitely sunshine music and definitely one with a distinct message. Within seemingly simplistic lyrics are some devastating truths, as with Buffalo Soldier. Listen to the words, understand the emotions. This is something close to genius at work.

September 2008.

Bob Marley has come to talk with me.

Bob says:

Although I wanted to come and be part of this book, it has taken me a little while to form my thoughts into something that people will want to read. They are not lyrics, which were easy compared with writing out my emotions in this way. But this is a chance I can't miss and I am glad and grateful for the chance to be known in this way, to leave a message for people to go along with my music.

First I want to say I am so very happy and pleased to find there is still a following for the music we created. It was a great, truly great experience to write and record the songs, the rhythms, and then to take that music out and perform for appreciative crowds. No one who came to our performances went away disappointed, we were sure of that. The group and myself loved those times, they were better than any high achieved in any other way.

When they told me I had the cancer and they wanted to take away my bad cancerous bit, I refused. Rastas do not allow amputation. But, in truth, I have been told since I have been in the Realms that the cancer had its hold long before it showed in the foot, it was already in the body and no amputation would have saved me. We have our time and man, that was my time. It spread fast through me, like a forest fire, burning all up. I could do nothing to stop it; the men I consulted could do nothing to stop it.

Although it was ended a lot sooner than I thought it would, I look now at your screen and see the honours, the awards, the greatness given to the albums and the songs. I see the following still and I know it was good. It was all worthwhile. I left something of merit for people to remember me. And now I am able to speak to you and be part of your book. This is an honour, one I did not expect, nor did many who are coming to you now for their words. We find it a tremendous honour and opportunity, for at no time have we been able to speak to our public, before now.

I want to thank all who have built websites, who have played the music, who have honoured my name and kept the message alive. To all Rastas out there, hold the faith. To all who still listen to my music, thank you.

What do I do with my time here? I help and guide Rastas who are sick and ill, who are suffering the cancer, who are coping with bad things in their lives. I work with them and they know me not but that is the way it has to be. Part of me will live on in the music. Part of me will live on here in the Realms. And a lot of me will be out there, working with Rastas. I can think of no finer way of spending eternity.

Riders On The Storm

James Douglas Morrison

8th December 1943 – 3rd July 1971

Listening to Bob Marley's music brought me Jim Morrison, don't ask… oh, and he asked for his full name to be put as the heading. I am always prepared to do what the spirit author wants. Within reason...

9th July 2008,

Everything seems to be happening. The wonderful thing is, if you are listening to reggae, as I was, and you are aware of Jim Morrison somewhere in your mind, you know it is not the music which has brought him into your memory, that's for sure. I just became aware of him and because he did not need to give me a song, or say anything, I just 'knew' he was there, I filled up with spirit tears. This happens regularly and is an indication of the intensity of feelings which can be built up by something as relatively simple as instant recognition. Most spirit people who come are overwhelmed by the fact that they are accepted without someone saying 'it's all my imagination.'

The Doors' music and I go back a long way; it – and they – is/are much loved. Jim seemed surprised that I love this track more than the usual 'Light My Fire', but this is the one for me, dark, brooding, sensual, the song has everything. And so does Jim Morrison. The feeling I have is that the Doors' music was iconic, even in a time when icons were springing up everywhere. The lyrics and the arrangements were atmospheric, even today I doubt anything is as evocative as 'Riders On The Storm', especially the tantalising and instantly recognised intro. When I played the track in my car, where most music is listened to, my head began to tingle wildly and if I had not been driving, I would have been scratching my scalp like a mad thing. I knew then that song was the right one for this section and even more, that no matter what surprise Jim showed at my loving this more than 'Light My Fire,' it was also his favourite. *(Confirmed.)*

Jim Morrison had everything: looks, talent, youth and fame. He rode his own storm, drink, and had his own demons, which he drank to overcome. The lightning which took him in his 27th year did him a favour, he says, because the only way for him was down from that point on. His live performances had deteriorated due to drinking problems, he saw no future for himself as a singer going solo, he only felt at home with the band but the band was half the problem, as it were. Although he loved the limelight, loved being the centre of attention, there was also an innate shyness to overcome and drink helped, but eventually took over. He denies he died of a drug overdose or a drug induced anything. He says he had a bath, drank too much, slipped under the water and knew no more until he arrived in the Realms. There is much concealed in his background, things he does not want to talk about even now, which were probably the real reason for the drinking, more than stage nerves.

The complex dark lyrics were an effort in part to release some of the demons, which is why some of them appear to be obscure and can be read many different ways. Jim himself does not understand why some of them were written but is content to have the legacy of music out there. He is constantly surprised at the people who make a pilgrimage to his grave and those who still honour and revere him as a performer. He is glad the music has lasted but surprised at his ongoing adulation.

On a personal level, I am thrilled that he came to speak with me. His was the first section to be written, he was the first to come and talk to me about his life and his death, his music and his feelings now. He came with that beautiful smile that changed his face; he came with a vibration that was almost serene, as he has found an element of peace in the Realms which he could not find on this side of life. The demons are conquered; the drink is no more. Now there is only peace of mind and quietness of spirit and soul.

I asked if he knew the Doors were something special in a time of great musicians and lyricists and he confesses, almost shyly, that yes, he did realise that and it was a real effort to live up to the fame which that 'being special' created. It put pressures on that he did not realise would be quite so crushing. It happened relatively fast, which didn't give him a chance to come to terms with it. He says that is why many people end up on drugs or drinking too much and die at an early age. They think they can handle the fame, fortune and pressures and then find they can't. The responsibility of being in a top rated group, of having to produce outstanding music and lyrics, of endless problems with record producers who want to do things their way rather than your way, made life extremely difficult. It almost hindered creativity in some ways.

Jim works from the Realms with those who are trying to create something different, something with a message hidden in complex lyrics, with those who are struggling to make sense of life through music. He says often they don't know they're being helped and that doesn't matter. It's good work and he enjoys it. He has welcomed the chance of being 'recognised' and accepted and says he finds great pleasure in being around me from time to time and associating with my companions, albeit they are from a time and culture different from him in every way possible. (If you can imagine dark brooding sensual Jim Morrison talking with a medieval earl who is wearing doublet, hose, boots and feathered cap, you get some idea of the strangeness that is my life. The fact they are laughing together and enjoying each other's company says a lot about the ability of those who come to me to become good friends within a very short time.)

Jim Morrison is always welcome in my life, storms or otherwise.

That'll Be The Day

Buddy Holly

13th September 1936 – 3rd February 1959

17th July 2008

It's like an itch that won't go sometimes, a name keeps coming, I keep saying 'I know Buddy Holly is coming, but when?' and then, as I am settling down to go to sleep on the night of the 17th July, I find myself saying aloud 'It's me!' I asked my companions who 'me' is - and then realised who it was, Buddy, all smiles and great happiness at being recognised and accepted. I spent the following day having "Rave On!" sung to me…

25th August 2008

After several visits, when he just came to be there, smiles and songs and feeling of happiness and contentment, Buddy has finally come to talk to me. What does his music mean in terms of my life? Sunshine, teen years, good sing-a-long and dance-to songs, big surprise and intense sadness when the plane crashed. As if a piece of me had been taken away. It stayed that way for a long time.

Buddy says:

I loved the music. I loved playing in the studio and the live performances were great, real highs then, getting so excited at seeing the kids so excited at seeing us. The guys were great, the Crickets played so well, couldn't have asked for a better group to work with. It's magic to me that they still perform, all these years on. I never dreamed the music would last, never thought of my legacy in that way. The film, "The Buddy Holly Story" is like a dream, it will keep my name and my memory alive forever in people's minds. I can't ask for more than that. No performer can ask more than that.

Personal level, when the plane went down, I was bitter and resentful and angry that it was over. I had so much to live for, my beautiful darling wife, my music, my friends, everything. I was bitter and angry that Ritchie and the Big Bopper went too, they had so much to offer still, everything left to experience - as far as Ritchie was concerned. But that didn't last; it never does, if you are of a light mind. Only those who cross over with darkness retain that bitterness and anger and resentment that it's all over. Some feel it's over too soon but it's all part of a great plan which we are unaware of, only realising that we are a small segment of it and that everything has its reasons. I know that in the time I was performing and writing and making music, I did more than many do in a great many years and I am happy to say that I am still pleased with everything I did, proud of what I left behind as far as the music is concerned. There could have been more, maybe some would say there should have been more, but as I said, everything is for a reason.

I chose 'That'll Be The Day' for my chapter heading but I'm undecided: Raining In My Heart is a favourite, too. No, leave it as it is, that was THE song that encapsulated our music, our driving rock 'n' roll beat, the one that got everyone singing at concerts.

It means a lot to someone in spirit to be able to visit a channel on your side of life and not have to go through the 'it's my imagination' bit to be accepted. Sometimes that puts us off and we go away to look for someone else to contact. Just being able to speak with you has made me very happy, to see the smile I get when I visit and to hear "welcome, Buddy!" and know you mean it, is additional happiness.

If my beloved wife ever gets to read this, darling, I love you still. I would have loved to have had more years, many more years, with you but it was not to be. What we had was special beyond belief. I treasure it to this day. "True Love Ways" was written for you and always will be for you.

Ever, your Buddy.

My Sweet Lord

George Harrison

25th February 1943 – 29th November 2001

July 2008.

George's name came out of nowhere one morning, as I drove to work. He has yet to get in touch. I asked if I should include a page for him and got YES. It is here and I await George's company.

It is a habit of mine to ask for confirmation when a name is given to me. The confirmation I sought this time came from my friend Lynne, who was downloading the music for me to listen to and draw each person to me. She commented that she was downloading Roy Orbison when she came across the Travelling Wilburys, featuring George Harrison...

September 2010

Today I have stopped at George's page. It's been a long time coming but at last George Harrison is here to talk to me.

George says:

Where to start? We've been sitting quietly here, waiting while I turn thoughts over in my mind... but I guess we start with the Beatles and the success and the money and the girls and the mad, mad life we lived. It was good, despite a few ego clashes along the way, but that's to be expected in a group like ours, four disparate people coming together to make music. It was a good life, lots of money, lots of fame and fortune and yet it left a bit of a hole in me, I felt there was more out there than I was feeling. It was partly that which made me turn to the transcendental meditation way of life and Hinduism as well. Whatever name we put on the deity, it's still God of some kind, isn't it? I found some peace that way.

Music, very, very important to me. Writing it, playing it, recording it, wherever and whenever. The best days were with the Travelling Wilburys. Now that was a class act if ever there was one! Tremendous talent, no ego clashes, just getting on with the work of making fine music.

What could I say when I got the cancer diagnosis, only it's been good and goodbye world. So that's just what I said.

Now? Working with musicians of all kinds, dropping in on old friends, jamming with friends who have joined me in the spirit world. No complaints, none at all. It was good, it is good.

Thanks for this chance to give you a few words. Hope the book does well. It should do, there's enough big names here to make it work for you. It's the least we can do for all the work...

Purple Haze

Jimi Hendrix

27th November 1942 – 18th September 1970

July 2008

I know Jimi is around me, he has yet to speak apart from telling me which song he wished to have as his chapter heading.

September 2008.

Jimi's was a genre of music apart in many ways, inventive, creative, informative, almost savage in some of his lyrics, ever captivating his audience and his fans. His guitar work was out of most people's ability, due to his intense devotion to the art. He seemed to pour all his life into the music and the lyrics, creating something that will never ever be forgotten.

I am very honoured that he has chosen to come and be part of the book.

Jimi says:

Faced with a blank screen, words sometimes fly out of the mind. I thought I had much to say but it has gone! Crazy. Let me talk this through then, see if it all comes back.

Music was my first love. Music and then more music. Creating it, writing it, playing it, recording it, doing live performances and seeing the crowd go wild, hearing your own songs shouted – it would be hard to say sung – back at you is something unbelievable. Only those who have experienced it know what it feels like.

As everyone knows, fashion was my second love, the chance to get out there and wear outrageous – to many – clothes and start new trends was something else. My music, with its powerful sound created half by me, half by the recording studio equipment, was different too. I wanted always to be different, to be unique. Thanks be to God I was - and I still am.

There seems to be some dispute still over how I died. I did not commit suicide. Let me say that from the start. I drank too much wine, I was sick, I choked; I died. I realised no one was doing anything about it but no one wanted to take responsibility. Foolish in a way, the responsibility was mine first and foremost. My fault I drank too much, my fault I could not contain it.

My subsequent fame has surprised me. Such honours, such recognition, it has been almost worth leaving it all behind just to gain it! Who knows how my career would have gone? So many have ended up with albums which flopped badly, with sales that were dismal, with record companies that dropped them. As with some of the other visitors, I felt overall it was better to go out in a blaze of glory than deteriorate. Some, the Stones, for example, have managed to keep a career going. Not all of us could have or would have done it.

In common with many others who have come here, my work from spirit to your side of life is with musicians, especially those who are prepared to push the boundaries that bit further, to create a new sound, a new look, a new type of music. Then I am there, working with them, and glad to be able to do it.

I am more than pleased to be able to be part of this book. Thank you.

Yesterday's Dreams

Lawrence Payton of the Four Tops

2ⁿᵈ March 1938 – 20ᵗʰ June 1997

19ᵗʰ July 2008.

I was a great fan of the Four Tops, especially loving their album Yesterday's Dreams, but it had been many years since I heard their music. I was somewhat surprised at first to find 'Yesterday's Dreams' being given to me this morning, followed very quickly by 'Walk Away Reneé.' I said, 'one of the Four Tops is with me, but as you were a group and not individuals…' which brought a huge smile. I checked Wikipedia, waiting for the name to leap out at me. Lawrence Payton's name leapt out at me. I am pleased to say his tremendous presence has been here ever since. 'Yesterday's Dreams' was my favourite on the whole album. Somehow everyone who comes knows which is my favourite song. They're digging into my memories!

August 2008.

Lawrence has been around me quite a lot; his presence is a most welcome one. I feel happy and want to smile when he is there; he has that effect on me. I have been playing their music quite a bit too and go cold when tracks come on where Lawrence took the lead vocal.

Lawrence says:

I finally got here, July 2011. Three years this one has had to wait for me to come! The pressure is on as she wants to complete the book and who wouldn't? It's a crazy but wonderful idea, put to her by spirit and she has worked hard to make it happen.

Four Tops. Four men singing together, four men who were and are eternally friends. I know it says it in most of the sleeve notes, but no one else did what we did, stay together over 40 years. But we did because we were as one. You know well that Levi could have gone and made a solo career, but he didn't. He said we were one and it stayed that way.

I loved it. First to last I loved it. Working on the arrangements to get the best out of the four of us, pushing ourselves more to produce even better tracks... the studio work, the live performances, you name it we loved it.

I was the first to go, sad to say, it all ended far too soon for me. Far too soon. Now only Duke is left and we, the three of us, wait for the day when we are reunited.

(Sitting On) The Dock Of The Bay

Otis Redding

9th September 1941 – 10th December 1967

August 2008

For the second time Otis' name has been given to me, this time with a lovely smile and a sense of great joy. Otis is a light, vibrant presence, as if his molecules are made of music. He lived and breathed music it seems, in every possible way.

He chose (Sitting On) The Dock Of The Bay as his chapter heading because, although unfinished and really incomplete, in his eyes anyway, it has become synonymous with his name. It was a new direction for him, one that would have taken him into new fields, captured new audiences for his very special voice and talents.

Since his death in the plane crash, Otis has been busy with rescue work of those who die in plane crashes. Unlike many musicians, he has not chosen to work in the music field, but to work with those who go down in a plane. He says only someone who has been through it understands the trauma - the sense of total helplessness as the great mass of metal stops defying gravity and falls like a stone to earth, or in his case, into water. There is nothing you can do, he says, you are confined in a huge steel coffin which is about to become that in reality. He did not drown, the crash rendered him unconscious and he was so badly injured internally from the impact that there was no chance of his survival.

His comment is, if he had to leave anything as his legacy, (Sitting On) The Dock Of The Bay would do just fine. Gentle, meaningful, catchy, instantly recognisable, he says no singer could ask for more than that.

Georgia On My Mind

Ray Charles

23ʳᵈ September 1930 – 10ᵗʰ June 2004

August 2008

Middle of the night thoughts, given the name Ray Charles, no song. I said 'thank you and welcome to my world' and went back to sleep.

Next morning the name was still there, coupled with a smiling presence and a request that his song title be 'Georgia On My Mind', his favourite. Mine too, I have to say, and again realised that my spirit visitors are tapping into my memories! Ray Charles, a worthy addition to this book.

Ray says:

Music was my life. With it and through it I could express all emotions, the entire range. There is nothing as evocative as music; it's a time machine all by itself. You hear the intro to a song and you are instantly transported to a time, a place, a person, a situation, instantly! Perfect time machine. Music permeates our souls, our hearts, our minds and sometimes our bodies. I know I moved from side to side almost endlessly when singing, because it is hard to express emotion when being still. People sway, people dance, people join in.

I came in the darkness, in your sleep time, so I could be sure to get through and give you my name. A car full of music and spirit passengers is not always a good time to approach you, although I know others have. Ah, but with what tenderness did you say 'thank you' and 'welcome to my world' before you returned to sleep!

Enough to make my old heart turn over and wish I had met you in 'real' life!

You are performing a service for us who wish to be remembered to our many fans, giving us a chance to thank you to those who recorded our music, who came to our concerts, who saw us on television, who heard us on radio and who appreciated our performances, those who bought our records and kept them in their homes to listen to over and over. To them we give our heartfelt thanks as we do to you for doing this work.

To all of you, may the music remain in your heart forever.

Singing The Blues

Guy Mitchell

22nd February 1927 – 1st July 1999

August 2008

'Singing the Blues' was given to me in the middle of the night, I went back to sleep again after saying "welcome, Guy!" and feeling that intense 'thank you' vibration which follows every time. Someone from the early days of my musical life, as it were, and a very welcome addition to this book.

September 2008.

My visitors come at different times and in all shapes and sizes, too. Sometimes they come quickly, very soon after giving me their name, sometimes they are somewhat later in coming, no doubt while they think about what they want to say. Guy came back within a month, much quicker than some of the contributors. I was about to start work on a book when I realised someone was here and was told 'one of those singers wants to come.'

Guy was a part of my finding out about pop music through Radio Luxemburg and the limited airplay given to pop music by the then radio stations broadcast by the BBC. "Singing The Blues" was a big hit and one I remember very well. I am delighted Guy has come to see me.

Guy says:

I almost fell into a singing career by accident. Singing was a sideline to earning a living for some time, but then it began to take off. I had different names, this one, Guy Mitchell, turned out to be the lucky one for me. 'Singing the Blues' was a big hit and made all the difference to the way people perceived me. I had the usual 'being accepted' problems that many have, especially those who write, as far as I can see.

I enjoyed my career, in all aspects of show business. It was a good, if risky life, never being entirely sure whether the money would be there to carry on a lifestyle that you had got used to. So the feeling was, enjoy it while it lasted and for me it lasted, I am pleased to say.

It has been very good to come and speak, to leave my words for the reader, who I hope will say: "I remember him!" rather than "Who?"

Final question, what do I do in the Realms. I work with severely disabled children, helping them regain their sense of wholeness in the spirit hospitals. It is rewarding work; I cannot imagine doing anything else.

Thank you to every fan, every person who remembers me and to this channel for letting me speak. It is a great pleasure to be remembered in this way.

Only The Lonely

Roy Orbison

23rd April 1936 – 6th December 1988

Roy came to me in the middle of the night as I lay awake thinking about the book and who else might possibly want to come. He came with "Running Scared" but he wants his most famous hit to be the one which heads his chapter. Roy is charming, considerate and talented and is a most welcome addition, as it were, to those who are coming to me for this book.

August 2008

Roy has been around a good deal, offering different songs, but the one he knows I like best and the one he says he likes a lot is "I Drove All Night". That one gets turned up really loud on the car stereo (sorry, people who have to listen to it as I drive by...) and I sense his pleasure in hearing the song. He is very funny; he makes me laugh.

I have had to wait until August 2011 for Roy to come with his message; I was beginning to think he had forgotten me!

Roy says:

Sorry for the delay! The problem is, as I know others have said, there is no time on our side of life and we tend to let things go drifting by while we get on with our spirit lives. The word has gone out, though, that this book needs to be finished and put out for the world to read, so here I am...

Good life. Good friends. Make that *very* good friends. Great pleasure in singing in recording studios, in working live, in working with the Travelling Wilburys, what a group that was!

And over before I knew it. A life of tragedies and good things, tears and sunshine, grieving and rejoicing. Extremes in many ways, but I would not have changed one part of it. Everything I did and experienced and suffered made me what I am now, a spirit with a lot of knowledge which I am passing on to those who need it even if they don't know they need it.

'Thank you' time. Thank you to all record company people who had faith in me, the recording engineers who helped make the songs so good, all family who stood by me, all friends who stood by me, the Wilburys who made me part of the group and gave me a life I will never forget, to all who bought the music and came to the concerts and bought the merchandise and made it happen.

And to this channel for accepting me. I have enjoyed being around you. I will be back.

Note: Roy has been back several times and is always welcome in my life!

You Send Me

Sam Cooke

January 22, 1931 – December 11, 1964

September 2008:

The name Sam Cooke was given to me in the same instance as Marvin Gaye. I commented; both you guys had a violent death, is that why you have come together, because you are friends in the Realms? Answer, yes.

Sam has chosen 'You Send Me' as his chapter heading. I look forward to talking to this great man of music.

October, 2008:

There is a distinct vibration when someone is ready to come and talk to me. This afternoon I felt it was Sam and he knows how welcome he is.

Sam's music was a pleasure for a great many people; the enigmatic 'A Change Is Gonna Come' has been said by some people to have been a prediction of his controversial death. But then, Sam's career was controversial in many ways, with his attempting to have a separate secular singing career outside the gospel one – and failing. No one could mistake his clear beautiful voice.

Sam says:

If the Lord hadn't wanted me to sing His praises, He would not have given me such a good voice, that blessing from Him I never failed to thank Him for. He also gave me a short life but a good one, filled with blessings in many ways. I sang, I reached people, I touched people and few, outside of those of us who sing, write or make films, can say that. It is a privilege and a pleasure to be His servant and the servant of the great demanding Music Industry too, for all that it brings its problems.

I see clearly that there are still theories and controversies around my death, so let me tell it as I remember it.

I met some dame in a night-club. She was doing the 'come on' bit and I thought what the hell, let's do it. I suggested a good hotel I knew but she said they wouldn't let her in and wanted to go to this cheap motel instead. I agreed because, well, I wanted to get laid and figured I would be out of there in no time. I wasn't planning on making a night of it.

But the bitch – excuse the word – turned on me, demanding money or she would shout rape and get me arrested. I went for her in my rage and she turned, grabbed most of my clothes and ran. I went to the Manager's office to complain and the damn woman pulled a gun and shot me. She must have thought I was going to attack her or something, didn't give me a chance to explain. All ended right there, cheap motel, dusty floor, stupid damn women who wanted more than they could have and assumed more than they should have. There, the truth is told. All the rest is lies and the world should know that.

But I know it was my time. When you get over here you learn about the great plan, you learn about how you choose the life before you come and live it and I agreed to do that before I came. I wonder why, even now, though, what part did that have to play in the great Master Plan that is the spirit council and the spirit world's responsibility to us? There is a reason for it, but I have no idea what it is.

I loved my life, my singing and my friends and family. It was good for as long as it lasted. I don't mind it being done too soon, as many say, thirty three's OK with me.

Here I work with people who have been shot. Simple, I do for them what they did for me when I first come home, because the shock to the system is pretty bad. A bullet hits you like a truck hitting you and it isn't much fun. I do what I can with as many as I can but it's getting to be a bit crowded these days with those dying from gun crime. And you thought the Wild West was bad…

I give you my thanks for this chance to talk about life and death, in this case, more death than life. Seems to me the music stands the test of time but the conspiracy thing about my death needs to be ended once and for all. It just hurts if it keeps right on. I'm here and I like it and I'm busy and happy and contented and singing in a gospel choir when we get together to sing His praises. It's good.

Dream Lover

Bobby Darin

May 14, 1936 – December 20, 1973

September 2008

Whilst driving to work, I told my companions I felt someone was around me, someone else to be immortalised. I knew the person was a pop singer, not one of the blues men or jazz artists. I had absolutely no idea who it was. I was listening to the Four Tops when the name Bobby Darin was given to me. I am very happy and pleased to welcome Bobby to the pages of this book.

October 2008

I was aware someone was around, someone who wanted to fill in the empty page of his entry, but that person was a little reluctant to come forward. I have been re-reading and smiling over the entries already here. Now I am at Bobby's page and it is he who is here.

Bobby says:

I was reluctant to come forward just now but should have realised, from the loving welcome I had when I told this one my name that I had nothing to worry about when approaching her for my part of this exciting book.

It seems like a lifetime ago since I began my career. It is a lifetime since I went home and have been very happy to be there, for life in the Realms is sweet beyond belief. There is work, there is play; there is singing and dancing and all manner of entertainment by those of the various professions who have joined the great band that is the Summerlands. I also work with those on this side of life who are incapacitated by heart conditions of all kinds. I had my share of heart problems. Now it's my turn to help others.

I tried to help others by donating my body to medical science. I felt it was the very least I could do then. Now I can do much more, although any medical research is worth doing, no one knows what might or might not come out of it. I may well have contributed in some small part to an ongoing search into the many diseases of the heart.

Going back to my career for a moment, I can say there's nothing like walking out on stage to a cheering applauding audience, to work with big bands, to have that massive sound at the back of your voice, your song, your performance. It lifts you like no other experience on earth, I am saying, because no other experience on earth comes close to it, apart from being an evangelical preacher and having an entire congregation held by your words. That is the closest I can come to an analogy. It was good, it was more than good, it was satisfying in a way that my soul needed at that time. I loved a lot, had a lot back; I gave a lot and got a lot back. It was a two way process that lasted until the final heart problem. I knew it would happen that way and am not unhappy about it.

For all the music, thanks to all who played with me. For all the adulation, thanks to those who bought the records and came to see me perform. For all the love, thanks to family and friends alike who gave it so freely. For the acceptance and the time to allow me to be part of this book.

It is an honour to be part of this project. It was an honour to be part of the great music scene during my life. I have much to be grateful for even now. If the small amount of help I can give to those who are suffering in this life is worthwhile, then I am happy.

Bo Diddley

Bo Diddley

30th December 1928 – 2nd June 2008

September 2008.

Middle of the night lying awake, thinking of not very much, the name Bo Diddley given to me and the sense of a presence of someone beaming so strongly I had to smile. His very vibration made me feel good. Bo Diddley's music had that effect, too. I fell asleep again, smiling, I do believe.

He is living proof, if that be needed, that people do not need to be in the realms for a long time before they can return and speak to us. June to September is a very short time in spirit terms. I am very glad Bo Diddley has been to make himself known to me. I look forward to his visit when he talks about his music and his life in spirit. I know he will be coming soon, he said so.

Bo Diddley is here this afternoon (same day!). He comes with the presence that is again making me smile and he is, as some of the other visitors have been, full of music. It radiates from him. His pleasure, his joy, was in making music and watching others enjoying what he did, joining in with his best known songs, sharing his pleasure in performing. It is a thrill beyond belief to perform, he tells me, to become one with your audience for a while, to hear the applause, to acknowledge the demands for an encore, to know they do not want you to leave the stage so you know you will be welcome if you are booked there again.

Bo Diddley says:

It was a full and rewarding life. Very full and very rewarding. I loved my music and the people who came to listen to me play and sing. I loved to make them dance, move to my rhythms. It is a pleasure to me that others have been encouraged by my work to become singers and musicians themselves. There is no greater accolade than that.

Yes, there was a heavy degree of racism in my early days. I could have been richer than I was but I was rich in what mattered, family, friends, love and ability to play. Could any man ask for more than that? I was shocked, pleased and honoured by the many who attribute their work to me, to call me the originator, who look to me as the beginning of their musical careers. It is good to be acknowledged, it is more than many receive during their lifetime.

I am content that I had such a long and good life, where so many talented and amazing people had their lives cut short by accident, drugs or illness. God was good to me and I am glad to be home in His world.

I am grateful for this chance to give my words to the people who will read this book. I know I came as a surprise to you, for I have not been in the Realms very long, but you were and are glad to see me and that was a surprise to me.

I want to say thank you for this opportunity. Now I know for sure that Bo Diddley will never be forgotten!

Monday, Monday

Cass Elliot

19th September 1941 – 29th July 1974

September 2008:

This month has proved to be very busy, spiritually, with visitors all the time.

One morning I heard the song "Monday, Monday" very clearly and asked who was with me. I got the answer 'Cass' and was filled with intense happiness at that moment, partly me, accepting another fine singer to these pages and also from Cass herself at being accepted.

That evening, as I sat circle, we became aware of a presence in the room and my friend Mary said she could hear something that sounded like "Sunday, Sunday". I realised it was Cass visiting the circle in person, as it were. This was very pleasing; it is not often anyone does that. She was - and is - a gentle vibration and a very loving presence.

Since that time Cass has been around a good deal, just to be friends, she said, to enjoy being a girlfriend for a while with someone who makes no demands on her. This is something I have not had up to now. I have a preponderance of males in my life; it is good to have a female friend to chat with about female type things. She often gives me the song "Creeque Alley" to let me know she is there, usually the lines "and no one's getting fat/except Mama Cass." It is fun and will continue to be fun until Cass decides it is time to move on.

I listened to a Mamas and Papas CD and also one of Cass's solo albums. Her voice is incredible, a true songbird with so much emotion in the lyrics. She is a great loss to the music world and a great gain for the

Realms. I am honoured and pleased to welcome her into my life and especially to the pages of Since.

The Mamas and the Papas were the epitome of 60s pop music, with more class, style and beautiful songs and melodies than many of the other groups. The intros are instantly identifiable even after this period of time.

Cass says:

From the group to my solo career, it was a wonderful life. Yes, there were moments of bitterness and unhappiness, but what life is perfect? Break-ups are never good, no matter who you break up with. But we, the Mamas and the Papas, had some wonderful times. Our recording sessions were a delight, we worked together so well, it all blended so well and the end result was, as far as we were concerned, perfect. I loved my solo albums as well.

I am enjoying my spirit life very much, if that is the right thing to say. I have been working with singers, ladies who are bigger than the average, ones who start out with that disadvantage but whose power and personality make them larger than life and someone to be reckoned with. It has worked well; many have made it big – excuse the pun – in the music industry.

It has been good to give my words to this fascinating book, a unique production, one for every lover of music. Surely it cannot be a failure! All of us who are in the book will have to work to ensure it is a success.

Just Walking In The Rain

Johnny Ray

10th January 1927 – 24th February, 1990

September 2008

There are many ways in which spirit let me know none of this is my imagination. I was having a conversation, late at night, with my Viking guide Thorbjold when I heard the name Johnny Ray being called alongside the words of my guide. Then you know this is for real. Johnny Ray is another welcome addition to the book.

I remember Johnny's music well from my earlier years and there was no question or debate over which song title would head his chapter. Charismatic, talented, Johnny Ray had many hits and even today has several websites devoted to his memory. Outside of this book, it is obvious many of the people featured here will never be forgotten.

Johnny is here tonight. Unlike some of the others, he has come to see me very quickly after announcing himself. I was told by Henry VIII, who was sitting with me that 'one of those singers, one of those people, is here to talk with you.' So I am taking time out from writing his book to speak to Johnny.

The vibration is energetic, happy; powerful. My fingers are actually tingling.

Johnny says:

I am so glad of this chance to say my words, to give this message to the public. I had a good career, chequered as it was with problems over my sexuality. I make no apologies for this; I just wish that I had lived in your

73

slightly more forgiving and understanding time. Whilst I appreciate that there is still prejudice, it is not as evident or as problematic in a singing career as it was for me. But then again, for each of us our lives can be a problem. It says much for my fans that they went on buying my records and came to see me perform.

I enjoyed my life. I loved to perform. I loved the accolades, the applause; the recognition. Whilst we all have to live and money is welcome, it is the rest of it which was my drug, my need. I am grateful to all who cared enough to be a fan; I send you all my thanks and my love for the support you gave me over the years.

I wonder if any of you recall a very funny sketch by Dickie Henderson when he impersonated me and my habit of constantly tugging the lead to the microphone. I smile now when I remember it. One of my quirks, to keep tugging the lead. We didn't have radio microphones then. Your new technology has gone ahead in leaps and bounds. It's something we watch with great interest from our side of life.

What do I do now that I am in the spirit world? As with others, whose words I have read on the computer screen, I work with singers who are making their way in this troublesome business, especially those who want to stand up and sing without benefit of a group to be part of, to lean on. It takes courage to do that. If I can help even one of them to make it as big as I did, the work will be worthwhile.

Thank you for this opportunity. I have appreciated being with you this evening. I thank you for breaking off from your writing. I bow with respect to the person sitting next to you and say 'Your Majesty, thank you for allowing me this time. I will now let your channel carry on with your book.'

Thanks to you all. It was good while it lasted and it lasted long enough to be really good.

I Heard it Through the Grapevine

Marvin Gaye

April 2, 1939 – April 1, 1984

September 2008:

The name Sam Cooke was given to me, followed instantly by Marvin Gaye. I am delighted and pleased to welcome Marvin Gaye into my world and to the pages of this book.

Marvin Gaye, an essential if not vital member of the Motown label. Big man, big voice, intense and sometimes sexy lyrics – his 'Sexual Healing' caused a storm, I recall! – and wonderful artist.

The song 'I Heard It Through The Grapevine' had to be THE one for his chapter heading, it's the one I feel is most closely associated with his name, outside of 'Sexual Healing' that is. It's an emotive and enduring song, which will continue to keep Marvin Gaye's name in front of the listening public for a very long time.

Marvin says:

For a long time the living was good! I enjoyed the music, the fame, even the infighting at the record company, where I had to stand out against company policy and get myself established my way, not their way. It worked, but it wasn't easy.

'I Heard It Through The Grapevine' was a turning point in many ways, a huge hit and one that actually meant a good deal to me. 'Sexual Healing' was even better, that meant more, I admit to being someone who loved the ladies, if you know what I mean.

My unfortunate death was to be deplored but – I had been ill with depression, despite the fame and fortune. Sometimes that plays a critical part in a depressive's cycle of ups and downs anyway. I went home and that was the worst thing I could have done. Being shot by your own father is tragic, as is the brain tumour they subsequently found him suffering from. A tragedy for the whole family. For me, though, it was a release. On this side of life I can work with singers and artists who are fighting their record companies, I give them all the strength I can and guide them to the right people to help with the fight. It works.

This has been wonderful, being recognised, having a chance to say thank you to all who bought my music and kept me going. If any of my family read this, then rest your hearts and minds. I did not mind, not really, not once I got here and realised how much better life can be and is. I am content. Not everyone can say that.

Grateful thanks to all who remember me.

.

River Deep, Mountain High

Ike Turner

November 5, 1931 – December 12, 2007

Middle of the night visit, September 2008, the name Ike Turner given to me very strongly.

I Believe

Frankie Laine

30th March 1913 – 6th February 2007

Frankie Laine came on the same vibration as Frankie Vaughan. It took me a few moments to disentangle them and realise two people had arrived together. Both are more than welcome, both come straight out of my 'young' life and bring their own memories with them.

My father loved Frankie Laine's music; we had many of his records, including the vivid 'Cool Water' which painted pictures in my mind.

My memories are of a powerful voice, evocative songs, clearly pronounced lyrics, delivered with passion and fire. The perfect combination for a star.

Frankie is a most welcome visitor to my world and the pages of this book.

September 2008

Frankie is here with me now, bringing his towering presence into my office.

Frankie says:

I was somewhat shocked and surprised when I saw the channel scrolling through my discography on her screen. I knew I'd recorded a lot of songs but that many? Absolutely amazing, a career lasting far longer than I thought it would, with acclaim all through, a dream come true.

Many embark on a singing career and in a short time find they are dropped by their record label, or the fans turn against them for some reason or other – we all know fans are fickle at the best of times –or the voice or the health fails. I kept right on singing and entertaining for a very long time. It was good, it was a most satisfying and wonderful life, one I would not wish to have changed in any way. That incarnation was just perfect from start to end. I would have wished for a better end, in some ways, the stroke left me feeling a bit fragile and for a man as large as I was, that bothered me, but to go quietly at the end was all I could have wanted really. I loved my family, my friends and my career. It was all wonderful.

It is very good to have this chance to say thank you to all who bought my records, attended my concerts, watched me on television or in any way showed their support for me. It is a strange relationship, the star and his audience, it is a symbiotic one, it needs nurturing and yet the star, the person, needs their privacy. Somehow the two must be balanced if the needs of the audience, the public, are to be met and yet the person retain an illusion of privacy. I think we managed it. I am grateful and honoured beyond belief at the accolades awarded to me during my life and after my death. I considered myself a singer, nothing more than that. The fans made me a star. I will never stop being grateful and humbled for that and by that.

I noticed other contributors have said what they are doing from the spirit side of life. I work with stroke victims. It seems a good thing to do, to help them rehabilitate themselves on our side of life – and sometimes we have concerts and we sing. I could not ask for more.

Answer Me

David Whitfield

2nd February 1925 — 16th January 1980

September 2008

Driving to work, listening to Elvis, knowing someone else was waiting to make themselves known to me. The name David Whitfield came through and later, when I looked up his many hits, Answer Me was the one he chose for his heading. David is most welcome in these pages. I remember him and his wonderful songs very vividly indeed.

May 2009

It has taken this length of time for David to come and speak with me, but as I worked on another book, I sensed his presence and heard his name. David, you are more than welcome to my world.

David says:

Apart from wishing to say thank you for the welcome and the acceptance, I wish to say how glad I am to be part of this book. To be remembered after so long is amazing and to see there are many who remember me still is even better. Somehow I got the idea that once I had returned to the Realms, no one would recall my name again. It is a pleasant and comforting thought that I am indeed remembered.

I enjoyed my career immensely. It was a good time, the gift of a voice that pleases is God given and I was aware of it and delighted to have it. Success with recordings was good, performing was better, that contact with an appreciative audience is everything, as I know others have said and felt during their time. Elvis I know loved to work with a live audience. I agree with him, there is no thrill like it, a big orchestra, a big backing, a strong song and the ability to sing it. Could any artist ask for more?

From this side of life I am working with young singers as best I can, as they need to be taught how to breathe as they sing, to make the most of the power of their lungs. When I am not doing that, there are many who cross over with heart conditions and brain haemorrhages and I am helping them come to terms with their new life, especially if their lives were 'cut short', as mine seemed to be, those who did not live to a great age. But, I know now that we all have a time to go home and that was mine. It is good to be remembered, I have to say that again, for it has been some time since I returned home and yet there you are, remembering me. Thank you all so much for the devotion, the loyalty in buying the records, those who are setting up sites in my memory, thank you thank you.

And thank you too for the chance to be immortalised in this wonderful book.

Green Door

Frankie Vaughan

3 February 1928 - 17 September 1999

September 2008:

Middle of the night, someone coming to me singing 'Green Door', could not be anyone but the suave, elegant, talented Frankie Vaughan, top hat, tails, patent shoes and huge smile, the one I am getting now as I write these words. I had to ask him to take the song away as it wound its way into my head and I needed to sleep… I felt rather than heard his laughter. Frankie Vaughan, straight out of my family life, a very welcome visitor indeed.

October 2008:

Driving home, I kept getting the name Frankie Vaughan so I knew this was the night when he would come and talk to me properly, rather than arrive, give me a smile and his crazy song and be gone again!

Although Frankie's trademark song is "Give Me The Moonlight, Give Me The Girl" he asked for "Green Door" to be the chapter heading as the song makes him smile even now. It is instantly recognisable – and intriguing. No one has ever explained the words and I doubt they will; it would take away the 'mystery' of the song.

Frankie says:

A mixed career in many ways, a mixed up life in many ways too, starting out to be a boxer, ending up being a song and dance man. Having seen how many boxers end up, punch drunk and out of it, I am very glad the pathway changed and I became an entertainer instead. It was a good life and I loved it. The songs were mostly American hits which I covered and had a hit with them here, which meant I must have done something right, added something, or my interpretation struck chords with the English record buying public. Only when rock came in did the career begin to slide but even then people still bought my records. It was a good life, as I said. I have no complaints. To be suave, debonair almost, to be able to dress in top hat and tails and look smart was something I liked to do anyway and to do it and get paid for it and to be able to sing and dance dressed the way that made me feel good, what more could any performer want?

My other work, with troubled youngsters, was even more valuable to me than the performing. You have no need to ask what I do from this side of life – the work goes on. There is a good deal of it to be done, never ending, in fact, as youth social problems are very much in your news today. I do all I can. It isn't enough and never will be enough but I do have others to help, those who have the same feeling about the problems as I did and I do, people prepared to spend their time working with the deprived, the outcasts, the troubled young people who need someone or something to cling to. If I help only one it will make the work worthwhile but I know there are more than that who are helped by me and those who work alongside me.

I want to say a very big thank you to this channel for working with me in this way. It is good to know I am remembered, that there are people still prepared to spend time creating websites and links about me and my work. It is good to know I will not be forgotten. I am glad of the chance to tell people what I am doing now. To all fellow Water Rats, if any of them read this book – and they will, dear one, I can tell you that – I want to say it was an honour to be King Rat. Keep on with the work, fellas, it's needed.

Chantilly Lace

Big Bopper (aka JP Richardson)

13ᵗʰ May 1941 – 3ʳᵈ February 1959

September 2008.

Buddy Holly came to talk to me, asking if Ritchie Valens and the Big Bopper could be included in my book. I said of course, they would both be more than welcome in my world and in the book.

Next morning I found, contrary to my usual practice of wearing my hair caught back in a barrette, I had put it in a ponytail. It was not until I was walking down the road to my car that I realised I could hear 'Chantilly lace/a pretty face/a ponytail/hanging down' … and then I heard the Big Bopper laugh and say 'You *know* what I like!'

The Big Bopper is inextricably linked with that song, which remains a classic to this day. A pounding beat, the simplest of lyrics, a song which winds itself into your head and stays there, guaranteed ingredients for a hit. But to make a record that survives ever changing styles in music and musical tastes needs another ingredient: an outstanding person to sing it.

The Big Bopper is a legend in every way possible, from his marathon broadcasting session which broke records, to his great often humorous rock-a-billy hits and style of playing. He is - even now - much missed.

JP Richardson says:

It is hard for me to believe that nearly fifty years after that plane crashed in that field - and I can tell you I had never been so scared in my life as when I realised we weren't gonna make it - my music and my name lives on.

Scared? Yes. We can all have faith in God, in the afterlife, in Heaven but when the moment comes, that moment when you know that plane, which defies all gravity to get into the air, is going back down where it should be, but much faster and with more emphasis than it took off and that you ain't gonna survive the impact, man, you're **** scared. But none of us got much time to realise what was gonna happen to us. Flying/not flying and instant death. One minute in a small plane, next minute a spirit looking down on the shattered remains of the plane and the shattered remains of my friends, too. Then I looked around and there they were, alongside me. I remember thinking 'Waylon should have been on that plane but God needed him on earth a bit longer, it seems' and then wondered why He wanted me home so soon.

I soon found out. I've been busy since I've been here. Apart from working with my son, who plays my music and impersonates me, I've been counselling, pushing, guiding and advising those who want to play music. It would seem, by the words in this book, that many do the same. Well, we're musicians to our bones, physical and spiritual bones, it is right that we give some of that back. Who knows how many we've helped, guided, pushed into new careers, ones that have become glittering stars in their own right, because of the work we did with them in the beginning?

Our sadness comes when some of those glittering stars fall foul of the terrible drugs scene and end up going home through that, those who had so much more to give.

But, it's not for us to question the great plan; it's for us to go along with the work we love to do, whether that singer or musician survives the course, the pressured lifestyle, is not for us to concern ourselves with. We do the work; we move on and help the next one and the next one.

The Big Bopper takes this chance to say "hello baby!" to everyone who remembers me and who goes to see my son performing my songs and to say thank you to them all.

2009

Catch A Falling Star

Perry Como

May 18, 1912 – May 12, 2001

February 2009,

Getting ready to go to work, an Elvis song in my head very strongly influencing all thought, when through it came 'Catch A Falling Star' and Perry Como had arrived. Gentle smile, loving presence, delightful vibration. Perry, welcome to my book.

Just one day later, Perry is here to give me his words.

Perry says:

There is a song which says "what a wonderful world" – I second that and want to add what a wonderful life. I had everything I ever wanted, all the recordings, the TV shows, the concerts, the fan base, the accolades, the family life, the friends and the sheer unbelievable pleasure of singing. There will be many among those who have come to speak to you for this book who will say the same thing. I believe those who come for the other sections, the country one, the blues one, will also say the same thing. When you have a voice that is a God given gift, one people appreciate and want to listen to, it is a truly wonderful thing. I rejoiced all my life that I had such a gift and I hope I used it well, that I did no one any harm throughout my career.

I am glad of the chance to be immortalised in this book, an unusual project, a very different concept and one that will attract a lot of attention. My thanks go out to Brian Jones and Gene Pitney for the work they do on our side of life, in seeking out and asking those of us who were not aware of the book's existence to come and make ourselves known so we can be part of it. I confess to a small degree of apprehension when I approached, but Gene insisted that provided I came with a song this dear channel knew well, I would be accepted and I was. I am!

Life on this side is good, there are many occasions on which we can sing and entertain people as we did before, there is an opportunity to work with upcoming singers, giving them the confidence they need to go out into the world and just sing. I do both and I find tremendous pleasure and satisfaction in doing it, too.

My thanks for the welcome, my thanks for making me part of your unusual book.

I've Waited So Long

Anthony Newley

24 September 1931 – 14 April 1999

September 2009

Anthony Newley's name keeps being given to me. I know this is the song he wants for his chapter heading. I now await Anthony coming to talk to me.

February 2012

Anthony is here. I have been scrolling through this book, waiting to see who it is has decided to come this day; I don't open this file unless someone does. Coincidentally, I had just looked at this heading and thought 'I have been waiting so long for this man to arrive...' and here he is...

Anthony says:

Apologies for the long wait! Has it really been that long? Of course it has, you had no reason to do anything but put the date when I first called my name for you to record!

What a life I had! From one thing to another, from acting and film to recording and writing and making hit records, no less. I loved it all, the ups, the downs, the excitement, the sheer fizz, if I can put it like that, of being involved in creative things.

The Strange World of Gurney Slade was, for me, one of the true high points of my career. Offbeat, surreal, funny, everything I ever wanted it to be, it was. And I now see that it 'is', too, available for the world to

90

buy and see all over again. My channel has been waiting a long time to get her hands on a copy so she can relive the magical series that she loved so much back then. Fifty years ago...

'I've Waited So Long' was a favourite for me, which is why I chose it for the heading on this page in this special book. I won't dwell on the passing; it was horrid, debilitating, painful and thoroughly unpleasant. My life is what I want to celebrate in these pages, a life of sheer joy, of entertaining and being entertained, of having an audience, a fan base and a living from that which I liked doing best.

Thank you for this time and for waiting so patiently for me to come and fill in this blank page. Every wish for your future, and many thanks to all who remember me and who listen to the music even now. I have much to be grateful for. And I am.

Blue Suede Shoes

Carl Perkins

April 9, 1932 – January 19, 1998

September 2009

Carl Perkins' name keeps coming into my mind and when I typed his name in for a chapter heading; *Blue Suede Shoes* followed automatically, no prior thought. Thank you, Carl. I will welcome your visit when you are ready to come and talk.

August 2013

I have learned patience with spirit; they don't come when I expect them to… as shown by waiting all this time for Carl to come back with his message. I have been scrolling through the pages this evening, hoping for a hint of who might come and fill in the blank pages.

Carl is here. Welcome, welcome!

Carl says:

I hadn't realised it had been quite that long… been too busy having a good time in the spirit world! So many people to catch up with, those who were already there, those who have been arriving since I crossed over, I clean forgot the years slipping away.

So, where to start? It was a good life, good music, good friends. Got to say the high spot, in some ways, was that gospel jam session with Elvis, Johnny Cash and the great Jerry Lee pounding the hell out of that studio piano. Man, that guy could make any old upright sing, if you let him on it! How we sang that day, not knowing that old tape be spinning round capturing it all, but right glad I am that it did.

I chose Blue Suede Shoes for my heading but I know well what the channel would have put, Matchbox. And damned if I didn't record that the same day we had that jam session. Must have been some magic going on at Sun Records that day.

Thanks to everyone who remembers me. Thanks to all the fans who bought the records back then. Thanks to family and friends, musicians and all. Thanks for a good life.

Thanks to this channel for patiently waiting. Not many more to go now before this book is filled. Then you can start on a new one. Right?

La Bamba

Ritchie Valens

13th May 1941 – 3rd February 1959

Buddy Holly was around, impressing me with his songs. I asked if he had come for a visit, he having already given me his words for the book and he said no, he had come to ask if Ritchie Valens and the Big Bopper could also come and be part of the book. I said both were more than welcome.

Ritchie came, briefly, and said he will return to talk to me soon, but he wanted to say this: if you're going to die, then do it with one of the most famous names in the music world at that time… it ensures you have lasting fame!

September 2009

Ritchie has come visiting tonight. It has taken me a while to reach his page in Since, I have been scanning through the other pages, making amendments here and there to my comments, getting them right, aware of someone here, someone who has been standing back and patiently waiting.

Ritchie says:

It has taken me some time to work out what to say in my message, my contribution, so there has been a long delay between my first visit and this one. I knew this channel would wait, as she has waited for others. She never pushes any of us as she feels it isn't right, we come when we are ready.

I loved performing. I loved recording. I loved the sheer act of making music, of feeling it all come together as one. To feel the rhythm going through you, to dance to the music, to sing, to be out there in front of people … every performer in this book knows the thrill of that. Whether they sang ballads or pop, rock or blues, no matter what it was, they knew the thrill of performing, of pleasing people, of hearing the applause, of knowing they had brought pleasure to people with their talent.

That was me. That was me in every way.

I loved Buddy and the Big Bopper, characters, both of them, true characters. Buddy was a superb talent in every way, Big Bopper, JR himself, was larger than life and twice as big. I felt so proud being on that plane with these people, my friends, I felt as if my life was about to take off, that my career had nowhere to go but up. I was riding a musical high and had songs running in my head at the very moment I realised the plane was going down. In that moment I knew it was over. If there had been time, I would have cried, but it was over too soon for that.

Regrets? We can't have regrets really on this side of life. We know it's meant, all passings are meant to be but sad, yes. I would have liked a bit longer, I would have liked to have experienced more of those wonderful gigs and recording sessions and times hanging out with musician friends. It was not to be.

This was meant to be. I work with young people breaking into the industry, even though, as others have said, they don't know it. I'm there, pushing and cajoling and inching them into the place they need to be to get the right contacts and the right contracts. It's a good job. I like it. The satisfaction when someone makes it big and you know you have done your bit toward that is tremendous.

Being here this night and putting these words onto the screen is also tremendous. It has been good. I give you my love.

2010

*W*O*L*D*

Harry Chapin

7th December 1942 – 16th July 1981

It's a hot Sunday in June 2010 – I have been thinking of
many things, but not of this book. Yet here I am opening
up the file, knowing someone is waiting to talk to me. I
have stopped at Harry's page...

Harry says:

It wasn't supposed to end like that, with a fireball and a
terrible accident and no one knowing if I was dead
before I hit the truck or whether I was alive and perished
in the flames. For anyone who wants to know – as if it
matters now – I'm pretty sure I was dead when I hit the
truck. My heart went into what felt like a spasm, I lost
control of the car and was enveloped in flames. Not a
good way to go and yet – I felt nothing so perhaps it
was.

I did feel it was all over too soon but in the time I
had, I left some music for the world, didn't I? Songs
with messages and a campaign against hunger, too. I did
all I could in the time I had. crammed as much in as I
could and that meant a lot of love, too.

This is a chance to say' sorry about the lifestyle' to
my family, if they read this, to those who put up with my
chasing from one gig to another, all the time spent
writing and rewriting the lyrics to get them right, the
recording time when I wanted it right and the fact I

97

probably wore myself out physically whilst mentally thinking I could go on forever, but we all think that, don't we?

The hunger is still there, people. Do something about it.

Thanks for this chance, I appreciate it and the fact you recognised me, accepted me and wrote this for me without a flicker of hesitation.

Respectable

Mel Appleby

11 July 1966 – 18 January 1990

At first I was dubious; did I really have Mel Appleby around me? Of course I did, the beautiful talented singer who went home way too early, depriving us of the surprising and dazzling talent of Mel and Kim.

September 2010: Mel is here this afternoon to talk to me.

Mel says:

It was all over too soon, but perhaps it was meant to be that way. I crammed a lot into my few years, enjoyed being a model and a pop star; enjoyed the fame and fortune, the attention, the adulation in some places. The one thing I can say is; it was truly great while it lasted. Not many people can say that. I see my sister is enjoying her own fame and is doing so much in the way of fund raising, too. That pleases me a lot, and I am sure she knows I'm there working with her on this.

The cancer was a nightmare from the moment it was diagnosed, I got through the first lot of treatment and thought I would be all right but no... like a fungus it had spread. I had no choice but to give in, you can only fight just so long and then your body says forget it!

I'm working alongside my sister and all who are raising money for the African Caribbean Leukaemia cause. All contributions gratefully received...

Thank you for this chance to be in your book. I am very pleased to be here, even more pleased that you recognised me!

Runaway Train

Karl Mueller (Soul Asylum)

July 27, 1963 – June 17, 2005

I cannot begin to count how many times Runaway Train came into my head over a period of about three months, without my having heard it anywhere. Finally I asked the question on Google, 'who sang Runaway Train' got the answer, Soul Asylum, went to their listing and found that founder member Karl Mueller had succumbed to throat cancer in 2005. Karl has been working very hard to attract my attention and claim his page in **Voices**. He is most welcome. It just happens I love this song, always have done. It's evocative and meaningful. I await Karl's visit with great anticipation.

September 2010

One day after writing that piece, Karl is here, pushing for attention, anxious and eager to give me his words. He is most welcome.

Karl says:

I have been anxious to have a mention in this exciting book since I learned of its existence, word travels fast among musicians and singers! And now I'm here, very pleased to be recognised, accepted and given this opportunity.

For me it all ended far too soon. I held the cancer back at one point and thought I'd make it but it came back and took me without my agreeing to go. Nothing anyone could do about it. What is pleasing is the amount of work which went on afterwards, the band still playing and pleasing people.

Before we got to the great albums, though and the award winning Grammy song, we worked, oh how we worked! Touring and more touring, singing and playing our hearts out for the fans, all that energy and enthusiasm and it never let us down once. It generated a fan base and we used that to make the good albums and the touring started over again. It was a good life, if you can stand everlasting being on the move, new faces, same faces, new stage, same music. It can do your head in after a while; you need to be totally committed to your music and your group to carry on doing it. That's why some bands last and others don't.

What I want to say is – we were giving out a powerful message in Runaway Train. Don't let it get away from you. Young people are still going missing, it has to be stopped. They have to be found. Too much heartache and agony and abuse going on, too much kidnapping and baby snatching and enforced prostitution. End it all, please. I ask everyone who reads this to do something, anything, give money to the societies committed to helping runaways or those who work with the children in their homes, anything. Do something.

Now you know why I wanted this page so much, dear one. Thank you for the opportunity, thank you for writing this, thank you for the compassion I sensed when you watched the video for the song and saw the names and faces.

Thank you for listening to me.

The Hippopotamus Song

Flanders and Swan

Michael Flanders, 1922–1975

Donald Swann 1923–1994

September 2010

Flanagan and Allen, Flanders and Swann, names out of my early years of radio listening. I am delighted to welcome them to the pages of **Voices.**

Michael says:

There are times when the right circumstances come about for two people to meet and create the perfect partnership for entertainment. Different, we had to be different to stand out. My being wheelchair bound was a start, Donald at the piano matched me in many ways, so it didn't seem that odd, not really. In any event, we quickly found that people became so involved in our comedy songs and monologues that what we were wearing/doing disappeared, fortunately. In an industry that does not always look kindly on the 'disabled', we always seem to have to work that bit harder to be accepted, this was a great relief and gave us confidence to go on with our act.

Donald worked with me in such close accord it was as if we had been together all our lives. We fitted together perfectly and are pleased to be able to say we gave many, many performances and entertained a lot of people. It also gave us a lot of pleasure as well as giving us a living. He has my thanks for his ongoing friendship and support throughout our time as a duo, and thanks go out to all who came to see us, who bought the recordings, who watched the programmes and who helped make us what we were.

Donald says:

Michael and I were a partnership unlike any other, in many ways. One sang, one played, both collaborated on the words and the music, there was no differentiating Flanders from Swann and in a true collaboration that is the way it should be. I enjoyed the work tremendously, it was good to be so well received by audiences, laughter is always a good thing and we played to many a laugh. Michael's disability did not cause us any problems; we were accepted everywhere we went and that is all that mattered to me. It was a friendship I cherished and always will.

Thanks to all who remember us, who like the music still, who are interested enough to read this page of your very different book, dear one. And thanks to you for recognising and accepting us, too. It has been good to be here and say this for the book.

Unforgettable

Nat 'King' Cole

March 17, 1919 – February 15, 1965

September 2010

Nat's name was called about a week ago and today he is here to give me his page. My memories of him are of this haunting song, the one he chose as his title and which sums up in its entirety the smooth certain singing voice he possessed and the charismatic personality he brought to his career. No wonder he became outstanding! *'Unforgettable'* and many other hits were part of my growing up. Nat is most welcome in my world and in the pages of this book.

Nat says:

In a time when us black people were not widely recognised – and I accept that in some places we are still not widely recognised or accepted – my career seems to have been outstanding. The singing came easy to me, the TV shows not quite so easy but I was very pleased to do them, so that others would learn that they too could become famous, could make their mark on the society in which we lived.

I wanted to make music from an early age, learning the piano, learning to sing, getting attention from the people who mattered. I did my best to fight the cause of racism, I would not go where there was a colour bar, regardless of loss of income from appearing in these places. That didn't matter, what mattered was standing up for black people, performers and others, in a world that didn't want to accept us. It worked, to some degree, I think I helped break down a few barriers.

Most of all I enjoyed the singing. I wish sometimes that someone had said 'give up the cigarettes, Nat, they're death to you,' but no one did. At that time so many people smoked, no one thought anything of it. I also have to admit that my three packs a day habit would have been incredibly hard to break... not to be contemplated! Better I had not started but there you are, I did and it took me in the end.

I am happy to see my work still continuing, the awards I have been given, the people still listening to my music and buying my records. It's good. Really good. I am thankful for it. And for the chance to be in this surprising book, too. Thank you for recognising and accepting me and translating these words. God be with you.

Piece Of My Heart

Janis Joplin

January 19, 1943 - October 4, 1970

The name Janis Joplin was called not long after my friend Mary mentioned her name in a conversation.

September 2010

Where I am used to people calling their name but not coming to talk to me for some time afterwards, Janis is here already, full of vibrant energy and enthusiasm. It is good to talk with her.

Janis says:

Oh but it ended too soon! In some ways, but not in others. Damn the supplier - I didn't even get a chance to appreciate the hit; I was gone! Must have been pretty damn powerful to take me out like that. Anyway ... drugs apart, drink apart – can I separate those two from my life as a rock star? Probably not. Big Brother and the Holding Company was a fine, fine band, one of the best of the time. We punched out that rhythm, those lyrics; we captured an audience with sheer enthusiasm and scored a lot of hits, a lot of success. It was good. It was very good.

One of the problems of that lifestyle, touring, performing, reaching that adrenaline high and loving it, is when you come off stage and start to come down, you want it all over again. Drugs and drink supply that, in different ways. I held out on one but not the other for a while and then fell into the one I held out on, drugs, and from then on ... well, it was heading to Death Valley, wasn't it?

When it fractured a bit, the Big Brother band not being too happy about its lead singer being promoted over them, we were supposed to be one unit, it got difficult but we made more good music and then it really did all fall apart. I saw some of the writing on the wall and tried to sort myself out. I guess I left it too late. I came off the drugs and drink for a while; I went back on it for a while. It had me hooked good and proper, one or other or both, no way could I give up both and both were designed to kill me in the end.

But oh it was good, everything from live performances through recording to TV programmes, it was good. I have no complaints. Just wish for a chance to do it all over again, if God would be so kind...

Thanks for the chance to speak, thanks to all who liked and bought the music, came to see us perform, supported us throughout. Thanks to the critics who were kind... to those who didn't get what we were doing, hope you understand now what we were all about.

Now to go see if I can have a chance at doing it all over again!

Walking Down Madison

Kirsty McColl

10 October 1959 – 18 December 2000

September 2010

Kirsty's name was called at the same time as Janis Joplin and, like Janis, is here very quickly (compared with some of my visitors) to give me her message.

Kirsty says:

If you're going to leave this life, it's not a bad thing to do, go out with a highly controversial accident! It's a way of making sure you are never really forgotten, but being in this book is also a good way of ensuring a degree of immortality. Thank you for letting me come and talk with you.

I had a mixed recording career, sometimes doing what I wanted, sometimes doing what others wanted, but in truth, what I wanted to do was sing and I managed to do that whichever label I was on at the time. The odd thing, to me anyway, is the one recording which will hold my name forever, the 'Fairytale of New York' one with Shane McGowan, which was tremendous fun to record and I am so, so pleased it is ongoing even now, a great favourite with so many people at Christmas time.

I am sorry I had to leave my family and friends so suddenly, it was my time, I had fulfilled my contract on your side of life. I would have liked a bit longer, but wouldn't we all, if we were truthful?

Thank you for your time, thank you for letting me come and talk with you. It's been good. When you hear that Christmas song, think of me and know I will be around. If you need me, just call.

Memories Are Made Of This

Dean Martin

June 7, 1917 – December 25, 1995

September 2010,

A whole load of names being called to me for inclusion in this book. Dean's is one of them. He is most welcome to the pages of this book.

Dean says:

As I was as much a singer as a film star, it was best that I give my communication to the singer's book and very pleased I am to be here too.

An up and down life, certainly at the beginning, when I really feared that I would never make the breakthrough I really wanted and then when it happened, when I met Jerry, the whole world seemed to open up for both of us. Record deals, film deals, night club bookings, they were all there for us and we began to earn real money. But I do have to say that when we were actually performing, the money, whoever was paying us, the audience, did not really matter, we were performing for ourselves. It was the same when I made my records, I made them for my pleasure, I sang for my pleasure and I am sure that is why they sound the way they do. There is a sense of intimacy about some of them, as if I am singing to just one person, when basically I was, me. It might sound egotistical, you might look on it as being that way, but if you can think of better way of getting the sound that you really, really wanted, then it is not something I ever found.

My film career was good, I enjoyed it all. Being with the Rat Pack was tremendous fun, a great life. I think that just about sums up the way it was, a great life. I fulfilled all my ambitions, to be a serious actor, to be an accepted singer, to have a TV show, you name it I did it. That isn't boasting; it's a fact that I was able to do it. And so when it was all over I didn't have any regrets.

Thank you for this chance to be in the book, thank you for listening to me and welcoming me. It is good to be remembered.

One More Mountain

Obie Benson (Four Tops)

June 14, 1936 – July 1, 2005

Obie Benson is the deep voice heard on the Four Tops'
recordings and a wonderful voice it is too. He is also a
charming and charismatic spirit, one who is always
welcome in my world.

Obie says:

The one thing about the Tops is that whilst it was work,
it was also a lot of fun. We recorded and we performed
as friends, not just associates. After so many years of
working together we were as one on all the musical
arrangements, the stage acts; everything. It made it easy
for us to stay together where so many groups and acts
break up, go their separate ways, often quarrelling and
resorting to litigation. Thank God there was nothing like
that with us. We were – well, as it says in
'Indestructible',

> *we are friends/we are brothers/*
> *always there/looking out for each other*

And we were, too. All the time.

I consider myself extremely fortunate to have been
part of such an influential but more than that, dearly
loved group. Every recording was made with our
devoted fans in mind; every performance was given with
all we had, so the audience went away feeling they had
really taken something their time with us.

Thank you for this piece of your time. I know
Levi's great towering presence is often around you,
enjoy his company, I did – and do – for he is one fine

man. May the Four Tops' music last forever and that many more will Reach Out for us as they did when we first began.

I've Got A Lovely Bunch of Coconuts

Alan Breeze

9 October 1909 – 15 January 1980

September 2010

Alan Breeze's name was called then, it is now November and he has come to talk to me. Alan, you are more than welcome to my world. I recall your voice from so many Sundays of listening to the Billy Cotton Band Show; you were part of my growing up, in many ways.

Alan says:

I must be one of the rare people who performed for many years, 36 wasn't it? without a contract. Just turning up week after week to perform on the show! It was a life I would not have traded with anyone, at any time, for anything. My father was an outstanding singer, I never considered I was outstanding but my voice was pleasant enough for me to work as a singer for all those years and to work on one of the most prestigious radio shows in radio history, too! Can any artist be so lucky?

Billy Cotton was – and is – an outstanding character, great fun, tremendous personality and easy to work with. The whole show seemed to slot together without any real effort and yet everyone knew it took a lot of organisation to get such a seamless product on the air every week. I am so grateful I had such a wonderful showcase for my singing and that the public liked it so much.

My thanks and love go to my devoted family and especially my daughter Michele for her work on my biography and to all my fans, all those who remember me with affection, thank you. It would have been nothing without you.

Need You Tonight

Michael Hutchence

22 January 1960 – 22 November 1997

October 2010

Michael's name was called. I am still waiting for him to come and talk to me.

July 2013

At last I know Michael is around! It feels like forever but for him, as for all spirits, there is no time, it might as well have been yesterday he called his name.

Michael says:

I thought it was about time I made myself known to this channel and got my message into this book. There are still some people to come, but at least getting my page done is another step nearer to publication.

All over and done in a moment of sexual madness. My fault entirely, my stupidity but ask yourself what you've ever done in that moment of sexual madness. I loved working with Inxs, loved the driving music, the power of the songs, the response of the audience, the adulation – the women, the money and the life. Loved it all, start to finish.

The big thing is this, though: would it have lasted, or would I have grown old and embittered because we didn't do it for the fans anymore, because they found younger, more energetic people... I won't ever know but I can say this, it was good and I'm more than grateful I had the chance to be in the spotlight for that time and experience all I experienced. They're good memories, really they are.

Thank you for the chance to say this, to say sorry it ended when it did and how it did but – in the final analysis, does it matter how it ends? I'm content with the new life I have.

The Boy I Love Is Up In The Gallery

Marie Lloyd

12 February 1870 – 7 October 1922

November 2010

Marie called out to me, asking to be part of this book

October 2011

It's an evening of 'late arrivals' – my third visitor from last year has come to see me! Marie, welcome, it was a surprise when you called to me and I am so pleased you are here.

Marie says:

I wanted to be in this special book and here I am. How different your entertainment world is today compared with mine! All electronic gimmickry and flashing lights, fancy tight costumes that hide nothing – we would never have been able to get away with it. Never! I watch and I marvel and I think, could I have done that? Difficult to say, isn't it, for I was then and this is now and the performers now are entirely different from those of us who trod the boards.

What I want to say is this: I ran into all sorts of problems for being what they called lewd and there are your women prancing around virtually naked and they don't get into trouble, not the way I did! All sorts of people protested about my songs, my act, but I didn't care, the public loved me and that's all that mattered to

118

me. I loved being out there, in the limelight, in front of an audience, hearing them laugh, cheer, join in, applaud, all of it was music to my ears. I'm an old time star joining in a book of new time stars but we all looked for the same thing, acceptance by the public of what we could do. Right?

That's it, that's my message for you for this book, dear one. Thanks for hearing me call, I wondered if you would recognise the name when I said it – and you did. I don't think anything gets past you as far as spirit is concerned, does it? You know us and you care about us and you welcome us and that's right heartening, so it is.

Thanks to all who hold my memory still, in photos and on this magical world of yours that you can call up in a moment. I am right glad to be there.

On The Rebound

Floyd Cramer

October 27, 1933 – December 31, 1997

November 2010

Floyd has been to see me. I am so pleased!

October 2011

Floyd is here... I know there is no time in the spirit world, but there is on this side of life and sometimes it feels like an age before someone comes back to talk to me for the book.

Floyd says:

Has it really been that long? I know, the others have said much the same... sorry! I'm also going to say what the others have said, it was good. It's the truth, for all of us. If it hadn't been good, we wouldn't have been there doing it. I got to play with some wonderful people like Elvis, that rare outstanding performer, and with names like Patsy Cline, Jim Reeves, Roy Orbison, the Everly Brothers... session musician if you like but well paid and most of all, a truly great life. I'm not saying I knew all of them would become household names, although I can say that about Elvis, but I sure knew talent when I heard it. Playing with them was a privilege as well as a pleasure.

When my little record went and bounced into the stratosphere for me, I was so pleased! I liked that little bit of tune and it worked well for me. Bit like being here tonight is working for me, bringing me back in touch

120

with the 'real' world, once my world. I now watch you all coping with problems of recession and all the rest of it and think, I'm better off here where money isn't needed and the weather's always fine and everyone is so damn friendly it isn't true.

So, thanks for having me to visit tonight, thanks for the page and the remembrance, thanks to all the fans and the artists I worked with for making it one hell of a great life. I love you all.

Reasons To Be Cheerful, Part 3

Ian Dury

12 May 1942 – 27 March 2000

I have had Ian Dury's name in this book for some time, without Ian coming back to complete his page.

August Bank Holiday 2010

I am aware of someone around me. As usual, when this happens, I go through the book and stop at the page I feel is the right one. Ian is here and I am pleased to talk to him.

Ian says:

Not a bad life, not a good life. Being crippled wasn't much fun, apart from trying to get people to accept you as a normal human being and embarrassing the hell out of them when it fails. If there's one thing I can't tolerate it's people's patronising attitudes. That's why I got mad over the Year of the Disabled. We're just people!

Apart from that, I was fortunate to be able to make music and be part of the music scene. There's nothing like it. Whether it's working with a live audience or your band in a studio; it's music and it's magic. I had a great bunch of guys to work with; I met a great bunch of guys too, like Jools Holland, for example, and all the others. I haven't forgotten any of you, believe me.

It's good to know the music tradition carries on, good to know my music is still played and appreciated, good to know I won't ever be forgotten. I suppose it was odds on I would get something like cancer, they do say the good die young, don't they...

Seriously, it was all over too soon but at least there's no suffering any more. I'm working with those who were crippled in their childhood as I was, those who can remember what it was like to be healthy and then incapable. It comes harder than being born a cripple, you know, much harder. I work with them on this side and on your side when I can. No rest for us, no rest at all. It's good to be useful and I can drop by and hear my music being played here there and everywhere. Couldn't ask for much more than that.

Thanks, Blockheads, honorary and otherwise, wherever you are. It was a good life while it lasted and I hold fond memories of your part in it.

2011

Baker Street

Gerry Rafferty

16 April 1947 – 4 January 2011

May 2011

I will wait on Gerry coming to talk to me. He is around, he's made that quite clear, smiling, happy, the depression and physical condition gone from him now. I'm playing his music and he seems content with that.

End of June 2011

As I played 'Baker Street' this morning full volume on the car stereo, I went cold from head to foot, especially during the guitar/sax solo break. I asked 'is this how you felt when you first heard the mix of this song?' and he said yes. Gerry is here now to talk, briefly, of his career and his passing. It's still new, raw and painful but much progress has been made through spiritual healing and it won't be long before he's whole again.

Gerry says:

It was a love/hate relationship. I loved the music, hated the travelling, the endless concerts, the whole thing attached to being 'famous.' I wished so much I could make music without going out into the world and promoting it. I realise that is part of the work, but it doesn't make it any easier, does it?

But the music was everything, to the point when I could and did overcome my dislike of going out and performing. The studio was where the magic was made, where hearts could be poured into the words and the sound, where the albums came together as if by magic, everything I had in my head right there on tape and then on CDs.

I am now very sorry I allowed the demon drink to take over, but how else do you fight the depression that dogs your days? The combination was lethal in the end, which is sad for those I left behind. But, having put that all away from me now, I can start a new life here in the spirit world, which looks as if it is going to be challenging, exciting and magical. I am ready for adventures!

Thank you for the welcome, the acceptance, the joy with which you listen to the music. I can almost relive it again through your love of the lyrics and melodies I created.

Smells Like Teen Spirit

Kurt Cobain

February 20, 1967– April 5, 1994

I'm having an on/off relationship with Kurt, if you'll forgive the expression. He came to be part of the book, then he changed his mind and said he wanted to tell his story, then that changed again, he couldn't face it after all, he said and we're back to a page in the book. I'm not surprised he couldn't go through with the task of writing his life story, quite a few people change their minds when they realise the intensity which they would need to delve into their innermost thoughts to produce something which had not already been written. Kurt could not and cannot, even now, endure that thought.

June 2011, Kurt is here tonight to talk to me. It's been a while since we met; I'm very pleased to see him here.

Kurt says:

Thanks for your understanding. I couldn't face digging into the whys and wherefores of my past, been enough people doing that, it seems, and coming up with the theories of why I did this and why I did that. What they don't seem to want to understand is: I'd been through enough, couldn't face any more, didn't want to face any more and it was time I departed that life and began a new one.

Gotta say this, I'm not sorry I did it. Thousands of fans were and what it did to Courtney and my family... well, I'm truly sorry about that but it was my sanity against their suffering. My sanity won out. I wanted to die knowing I was sane. I wouldn't have been much longer if I had lived on, that's for sure.

Enough of the misery side of it: what I want to say is this: Nirvana was good. Really good. The music resonated through me and round me and – it was everything I ever thought it would be. That Unplugged we did still knocks me out when I see people watching it – and I do, believe me! I come and stand by you when you watch it, all you Nirvana addicts out there!

I'm pushing and shoving new rock musicians to get them on course for a career these days. I like it, I don't have to work all the time, I can hang out with others who are here doing much the same thing if I want.

Thanks to all of you who made Nirvana what it was – a giant in the grunge world. Thanks for this chance to talk, too. Appreciate it.

No Regrets

John Walker

12 November 1943 - May 7, 2011

Last day of July, downloading No Regrets and, whilst wondering why the impulse was there, I dissolved into floods of tears as the song started. John is here and the tears are flowing. Healing tears.

August 14th 2011. John is back to give me his message.

John says:

It was a good life. All round and in every way, when I look back on it, it was a good life. Being part of the Walker Brothers was quite simply amazing. No other word will do it but that one. We were idolised, we were courted by record companies; we sold millions of copies and became truly famous. Our songs live on; our voices are out there still. I would wish, more than I can tell you, that Scott would use that incredible voice of his to please his fans but that is his decision, one I cannot argue with, certainly not from this side of life!

No regrets. No, I have no regrets apart from the obvious one: that it all ended too soon for me. I wanted the suffering to be over, but I wanted it to be over and be cured. Accepting your forthcoming death is not easy when there is still so much to live for, family, friends and the sheer joy of living.

This is a perfect and wonderful chance to say thank you to all Walker Brothers fans, then and now, thank you for keeping us in business then and buying and listening to our music now. It is so good to know we will not be forgotten.

Never Say Never Again

Phyllis Hyman

July 6, 1949 – June 30, 1995

August 2011.

Phyllis came to me via the wonderful collaboration she did with Levi Stubbs of the Four Tops, singing Maybe Tomorrow. This is on a Four Tops album not released on CD (as far as I know). It's a favourite track, the sheer clarity and beauty of her voice is stunning and blended with the power of Levi's magnificent voice, this is really is 'once heard, never forgotten'. For me, anyway! It was shortly after I really listened to this track that Phyllis came to me, bringing her brand of beauty and gentle vibration.

Phyllis says:

I wrote on my goodbye note that I was tired, so tired. And I was, tired of all the pressures, of all the memories, the bad things more than the good ones. Yes, it's sad, yes, some people can cope with it, but I couldn't. Please don't blame me for walking out on it all.

But oh, the good thoughts! The good times, the sounds of a perfectly crafted song, like the one which brought me to this channel's attention, an unbelievable and unforgettable recording session that brought me so much pleasure.

The career was good, the music was good; the fans' attention was good. Underneath it was the heartache and loneliness that accompanies so many of us who live that life, the public life, the way the press watch every move, every outfit and every companion. I could not go on. I don't know why and I don't know, even now, how I coped with it as long as I did. Depression is the most deadly of conditions, it is invasive and intrusive and destructive. There are many in this exciting book who will testify to the truth of that statement. For those with depression often turn to drink and the two together are lethal. I am sad it ended, I would have wished to go on, but –

I'm happy now. I'm released from all demons, all depressions, all pain and hurt. There is joy in that and in working with people who succumbed to the awful cocaine addiction. Been there, as they say, done that. I can help and I do.

I want to thank all who believed in me, who let me sing, who let me soar to those giddy heights of pure magic when the song came together and the result was amazing. At times like that I truly lived.

The Night They Drove Old Dixie Down

Richard Manuel

April 3, 1943 – March 4, 1986

My first visitor in 2012, Richard Manuel, was a member of the highly acclaimed group The Band. After what seemed like months of being given the song Richard chose for his page, I bought the CD (again) and became aware of his presence when that song was being played.

Richard had a rough time in life, outside of the music, which he loved, and is still having spiritual healing in an effort to come to terms with that particular incarnation. As has been said elsewhere in this book, different souls need differing lengths of time to recover from the life they had here. He is around a good deal at this time, which pleases me; I love my spirit visitors. He is welcome to stay whilst he learns from my companions how to fully enjoy the spirit life and eventually to find the work he really wants to do.

Richard says:

It is a year on from when I told this dear one I was around her, through this song and others that The Band did. She has the film, The Last Waltz, several of us sat and wept quietly throughout it, all over too soon for so many of us there, the group and the guests we had for that final performance. What a time that was! What a life that was!

But it was all too much for me. Some of us aren't strong enough in our hearts and minds to stand the pressures of life. I was one of them. I admit it was a bad way to leave, but I couldn't face staying. Now I have a niche for a while, for as long as I need, playing music with some of the other musicians who have found their way to this one's spiritual home and heart. I'm healing through music and through the counselling I receive from those who are there to do just that. It isn't harps and clouds, people; it's Life with a capital L. It's counselling and motivation and finding your own way forward as we all must do. I'm not going to go all spiritual on you, though.

The Band was tremendous. It was a gathering of true musical geniuses in our field, the rapport was amazing, the sex, drugs and rock 'n' roll was something else. Anyone who tells you otherwise is not telling the truth. It was a time in itself, a time that wrapped you around in its tentacles, take this, try that, bed that and we did, over and over and over. I have the memories tucked away and indulge myself from time to time by going over them. I've met up with Levon and he's fine, in case anyone needed to know. We play together a lot now, making our special music for those who want to hear it.

Thanks to all fans of The Band, to Bob Dylan and all. It was good while it lasted.

I Will Always Love You

Whitney Houston

August 9, 1963 – February 11, 2012

It is the 13th February 2012. I am recording now that on the 12th February Whitney came to me, full of life and energy, sparkling with myriad spirit lights, to let me know she was alive and well. I have never been quite that cold, head to foot cold, in a car warmed by the heater being full on, assisted by the fan! She said she would be back with her message very soon, after I asked her to be sure to go for spirit healing.

The next day, a friend wrote 'I could have done without Whitney singing to me all night because an unhappy medium on the Isle of Wight told her to!' I had not told my friend of her visit...

It is the 23rd January 2013, not exactly 'very soon' but there is no time in the spirit world! I am aware of a large presence in my room this night and have returned to Whitney's page for her message, knowing it is her delightful vibration I am feeling.

Whitney says:

It's hard to realise it is that long since I came, that long since I left your side of life and emerged in the sunshine and beauty that is the spirit world. Suddenly all that bothered me fell away, all the problems, the stress, the hassle and the pressures. I was overwhelmingly sad for some time, in your terms, at having to leave so many loved ones behind but that is the way of it. I know some of you will want to know did I die by accident or design and have to say that is one thing I am not going to tell you, because there are investigations and it is not for me to get in the way of them, or to bring calumny on the head of this dear one channelling me at this time. She will have enough scorn poured on the work without that.

Let me just say I was welcomed, I am welcomed and it is good to be here with such warmth and acceptance. I had a wonderful time during my life, mostly, underneath it was not always so good but the one balanced out the other. I was sorry it ended but am delighted with my new life. I can sing and be myself here and no one questions anything. No interfering press but all the fandom I could wish for, so many fans are here and welcoming and wanting me to sing.

For all of you left behind who mourn, who miss me, let me reiterate, *I will always love you.*

And thank you for being there for me for so long.

I Feel Love

Donna Summer

December 31, 1948– May 17, 2012

19th May and I am aware of Donna Summer around me, full of life and smiles and energy. I said her name aloud and went cold from head to foot, just as I did when Whitney came. 'I will be back!' she tells me.

February 3rd 2013

Usual strong impulse to go to this book and not the one I am currently writing. Donna is here; full of smiles and energy just as she was when she came the first time.

Donna says:

We would like this book to move on, to do that we need to come with our messages! So here's mine. Great life, with all its ups and downs, fans and critics, loves and hates. To walk in the spotlight of fame for a short while is something you never forget. To have a wonderful career like mine makes that life so worthwhile. To know people bought the records and enjoyed the music and the performances means everything to me.

I don't know yet what I want to do in the spirit world, whether I want to come back and start a new life, no idea, still enjoying myself at the moment. I doubt anyone would begrudge me that!

Just want to say thank you, thank you to all who worked with me, all who liked the songs, all who came to the performances, all who had any part in my life, and made it what it was. Memorable.

Massachusetts

Robin Gibb

22 December 1949 – 20 May 2012

Today, 30th July, 2012 I shared lunch time with Robin, who came as a powerful, almost overwhelming presence of lightness and joy. He is more than welcome in my life.

August 22nd, 2013
After what feels like an eternity of waiting, with Moody Blues on my earphones, Robin has arrived. I need to mention something here before we go on. I told my partner Terry on the 30th July last year that a new spirit was around me. He said, 'it's our Robin.'

Robin says;
With the soaring strings and haunting melody of Nights In White Satin echoing round my channel's head, I come to give my message to my fans. Apologies for the long delay, spirit life is exciting, interesting, varied and we tend to overlook small things like time... which slips away so easily.

I had a good life. I had an incredibly busy life, so much writing, so much music, so many influences, hard to name them all, so let me say they were there. My brothers, my dear brothers, my family, my fans. All appreciated beyond my ability to say anything about them, but they know how I felt and how I still feel about them all. The music was everything. Making it, writing it, singing it, working with it. What an industry! Is there anything so wonderful as a song which acts like a time machine, taking you straight back to the moment you first heard it? Nothing else does that. Perfume comes close but nothing equals music.

The illness which took me was an enemy. I fought it but it conquered in the end. It always does.

Thanks to everyone for giving me a truly wonderful life. I hope the next one can be as good.

The day I had lunch with the channel and her partner was wonderful. For a time I was a real person again, albeit invisible and unable to speak to all who were there. But the two people I was with knew I was there and the love that swept over me was indescribable. Thank you for that. Thank you from the bottom of my heart. It meant a lot. It still does.

No Rain

Shannon Hoon (Blind Melon)

September 26, 1967 – October 21, 1995

December 2012

I have been persistently given the Verve song with the line 'the drugs don't work' and asked who was with me. I got my answer: Shannon Hoon, who is more than welcome in my book and in my life. He is a smiling, beautiful, serene presence.

November 2014

And here I am, persistently being given the Verve song with the line 'the drugs don't work' and once again Shannon Hoon walks into my life, as smiling, beautiful and serene as before. This time I hope he's staying long enough to give me a message!

Shannon says:

I hadn't realised how long it'd been, but there I was with the same song and the same instant recognition of someone who wasn't that well known, not really, not a household name.

And yet, looking back, I had it all, didn't I? Big name bands wanting me to record with them, big recording contract, big future. Songs to be written, songs already written, everything was there for Blind Melon to be one of the big stars. And I blew it – ha! Bad pun there. Cocaine put a stop to it all. The drug therapists didn't cut it with me, no one got to the reasons because I didn't know the reasons. If I had, I could have done something about it.

The touring was fantastic. The audiences were great. I loved it all, the whole performance thing, even if it was clouded by the big C at the time. It was still good. I have a ton of fantastic memories to look back on from this side of life.

Mostly I want to say sorry to the guys in Blind Melon, not good for them, it was their career I cut short as well as my own, wasn't it? I want to say sorry to Nico and wish I could have stayed around on your side to see her grow up into the fine woman she is now. Sorry to my family for giving them the burden of bereavement. Sorry to the fans who lost out on some good Blind Melon stuff and hope you go on liking what we did when we were together.

Nice gravestone I have, appreciate that, people. Very nice.

Life was nice - with and without.

Thanks to this channel for recognising me twice and for listening to me today. This book is coming to its end now, isn't it, as the last of us laggards finally make it back to give our messages to her.

You're great, all of you. Thanks again for making it good whilst it lasted.

Tulips From Amsterdam

Max Bygraves

September 26, 1967 – October 21, 1995

27th December 2012 and Max Bygraves has announced himself as being here. I hope to talk with him very soon.

21st October 2014
Max is here tonight; his smiling presence cannot be confused with anyone else.

Max says:

Not exactly soon… but I'm here at last! Not only for this, but you know that, OK, so I've arrived and to prove it, I'm 'ere…

It was a good life, and a long one. I nearly made it to 90, didn't I? Close enough anyway. Did a lot of things, met a lot of people; loved a lot of people. All those Royal performances, right honour that was, I can tell you. All that singing, oh I loved to sing, loved making records, loved the thought that people had my music at home and were playing it and singing along with it, the lyrics weren't difficult, were they? Just loved it all. Start to finish. America, UK, wherever. Loved it all.

Thanks to all the Water Rats, all the people I met who became friends, no matter which side of life you're on, thank you. Thanks to all the fans that came to see me and bought the records. I wouldn't have got there without you, would I? Thanks to all the people in the TV world who made the magic happen. Needed them too.

Thanks to this one for letting me be in her book. She's a hard worker for spirit and we give her our thanks and admiration for all she does.

The Days Of Pearly Spencer

David McWilliams

July 4th 1945 – January 8th 2002

19th February 2013 – the name David McWilliams is called. I welcome him to my world.

It's the 24th August 2013 and David has been giving me his mysterious and haunting Pearly Spencer song. David is here with his message for his fans.

David says:

Too soon, it all ended much too soon! What sort of age is 56? I had much I wanted to do but – it ended and there is nothing anyone can do about it but accept. It has taken me a while to do that but now I am capable of looking at it and thinking, there's a lot of great singers/songwriters/musicians here in the spirit realms who crossed over a lot earlier than I did and they too had much they wanted to do. So... I quickly stopped feeling sorry for myself and began making contact with everyone I knew and a few I didn't. We are a big crowd of musically minded people here and it's fantastic. We make music like you would not believe.

Thanks, loads of them, to all who supported me throughout my career, family, friends, fans; all of you are simply wonderful. It's good to have a chance to say thanks, it all ended so fast there wasn't much chance back then. I just looked, has it really been eleven years since I crossed over? It seems like yesterday and yet it feels like forever.

Stay strong, stay well, and thanks again to you all. You made it a life I am pleased and proud to remember.

We've Only Just Begun

Karen Carpenter

March 2, 1950 – February 4, 1983

Karen Carpenter arrived in my life 25th August 2014, with all the delicacy and vibrancy of a summer flower.

The day before Karen arrived I had been migraine sick, so when I felt sick again, I thought it was that returning. Then I got Rainy Days and Mondays... and the whole thing fell into place. The beautiful, fragile, delicate Karen was here - and how! We watched a couple of videos on Youtube, with Karen bringing tears to me as she watched her once lovely self performing, confirming over and over that she is really there. Her tears came most strongly when there were close-ups of her brother Richard on the screen.

Karen has said she will be around for a while. I do hope so, this is one lovely lady. She is not yet ready to leave her message, one step at a time, she says.

Karen never returned to give me a message. I have deleted a few names from these pages where the promised visit never happened, but in this instance, I have a little more to put in her page as we watched the videos together. If I do another book and Karen wants to come, I will welcome her.

Waiting At The Church

Vesta Victoria

1873-1951

December 2017 and that old music hall song has been in my head for an age. Then Vesta visited to tell me she was once as famous as Marie Lloyd, she says all music hall ladies were famous because of their 'reputation' of being on the boards, she just happened to have a song that has endured through the years.

Vesta says:
I loved my life! Loved the elaborate clothes for the stage, the outrageous makeup, the fact you can be many times the size of your normal self when out there parading yourself up and down the boards, stamping out the rhythm of some silly song and hearing the roars of approval from the (mostly male) audience. That's audiences here and in the States. Oh, they liked a bit of music hall over there, you know! I watch your singers today, wondering what they would do with 'Daddy Wouldn't Buy Me A Bow-Wow' or 'Waiting At The Church' come to that. Only your clever Lonnie Donegan managed to make a success of comedy songs over and over again after us music hall people weren't in demand any more.

But this is my bit, and I want to say it's good to be remembered. Not many of you scanning through this book will remember my name, they might remember the song, though, it was sung in many a public house when the drink had flowed enough! So here I am, Vesta Victoria, Baby Victoria if you like, imagine me singing at four years old!! Asking you not to forget me and the other music hall stars of our time. We were the equivalent of your famous faces on TV now and we gave a lot of pleasure to a lot of people.

What do I do now? Nothing much, if there's a wannabe music hall star practicing I drop in and give them a hand, there are some who like to recreate the old days, otherwise I'm – well, being lazy but I have plans…

Thanks for talking to me, dear one.

Maybellene

Chuck Berry

1926 – 2017

8th April 2018

I was woken in the night by a door slamming, as if a draught had caught it. There are no closed doors in my home… and the cats didn't panic so it was a spirit induced sound. So the inevitable question, who caused it? Who wants my attention right now?

A day later and I am thinking 'Chuck Berry' even as I'm listening to and singing along with Elvis. That's when I know for sure it isn't my imagination…and thought, yes, it's the sort of thing Chuck would do to get attention…

Chuck says:

How did I make it to 90? With my lifestyle and the energy I used up performing, but there you go, I did and right pleased I am to have made it to a good age, where so many have gone much, much younger than me. And yes, it was me slammed the door, but then I'd thrown my name into your head several times and it went nowhere! Trouble is, apart from dying, what had I done in my later years? Nothing much, so I rather slipped out of the limelight. I didn't care for that, but there wasn't much I could do about it.

I did spend time thinking about the performances, the recordings, the way I was treated by others at that time and thinking how easy it is – in a manner of speaking – to be 'different' in your world today. Seems to me the problem you people have now is with the gay community while you're accepting us, so there will always be a problem. I can imagine a prejudice against robots in the future – at least they won't be sentient, which is just as well, considering the way you're going today.

Enough of lecturing, but thanks for the chance to say that, been wanting to say it for a while. I had a good life, taken overall, made money, made music, made pleasure for thousands, can't be bad, can it? And before you ask, I'm right there behind the new talent coming along, the ones who want to make fast paced music with strong lyrics and a pounding beat. You'll know it when you hear it and you'll think of me. I hope.

Thanks for fitting me into this book. I would have hated to wait for the next one…

Thriller

Michael Jackson

August 29, 1958 – June 25, 2009

It's the 7th May 2018 at a point when I considered this book more or less closed, with 'new' names going into Voices II. Then I heard the name Michael Jackson being called and the comment 'I want to be in the first book!' It's not in me to say no to any spirit, so here is Michael's entry in Voices. I had been hoping he would come; it is a pleasure to say he's here.

Michael says:

Yes, I could have waited for book II but having made up my mind I wanted to be part of this, well, I wanted to be in the first one. So here I am…

What a roller coaster of a life – what strange experiences, outside my head and in it, what riches and then worries about riches, what fame and then worry about keeping that fame, putting everything into new work, new songs, new routines and all the time wondering why the little voice in my head was saying 'keep going, Michael, keep going, the time is running out fast'. And it did. I was there, I was not there. I would ignore the voice at times and listen to it at others. I did a lot, didn't I? Gave you masses of great music, including Thriller. I couldn't pick one song, so I put that there instead. You all know the success of that record, even now, everyone knows it.

I seem to be rambling a bit, but that's fine, others have done the same, I know that, I've peeked at the other entries in this book. My career was tough going at the start with the 'encouragement' of my father, trying to

148

make the Jackson Five the biggest thing ever. We did, didn't we? So my solo career was more or less given to be a success. I am proud of that, proud of the work I did, the songs I gave you, even if it all went a bit strange at times. Only now, looking back on it all, can I see how strange it all got and wish I could do something to straighten it out. Too late, we only get one chance at a life.

Thank you to every fan, every critic, every editor who mentioned me, bought the records, went to the concerts, followed my career, talked about me... it ensured I'd not be forgotten then and now, being here, I can be sure I won't be forgotten in the future, either.

Thanks for doing this for me. Now you can finish the book... (laughs)

SECTION 2 – COUNTRY ROADS

With the assistance of Johnny Cash

Johnny Cash, *Ring of Fire*
Freddie Fender, *Before The Next Teardrop Falls*
Roger Miller, *King of the Road*
Charlie Rich, *Behind Closed Doors*
Hank Williams, *Your Cheatin' Heart*
Faron Young, *It's Four In The Morning*
Tennessee Ernie Ford, *Sixteen Tons*
John Denver, *Take Me Home, Country Roads*

So here we are, September 2008, beginning the section for some of our much loved C&W singers, beginning with the Man In Black himself. Where else could he be?

Ring of Fire

Johnny Cash

26th February 1932 – 12th September 2003

June 2008 - I am aware that the C&W legend Johnny Cash, the Man in Black, is around. I know he's there, I sense his presence but as yet he's not coming close to speak with me. I have ordered and am awaiting a CD of his later material, which he has indicated will be better for me to understand why he is coming.

The CD contains the song 'Hurt' which immediately gave me problems, in that I would fill up with tears each time it came on. It climaxed, as it were, one Sunday when I sat in my car in the car park and broke down completely. After that the song could play without any tears at all; it is as if whatever demons Johnny had expressed in his version of that song had finally been washed away by my tears.

I call this great man Mr John, a more respectful title in a way than Johnny. I find him powerful, intense, emotional and devoted to those he loves and his music.

28th September 2008

John has been around both my friend Lynne and me this Sunday morning. He visited Lynne to say he liked the idea of the book and to propose the title, Country Roads, which is what it will be called.

He then came to me to say thank you for the tears through the song 'Hurt' and that it had helped a lot. That's all I needed to know. Any amount of distress is worth it as long as it helps the person who is suffering so much still. Demons are being chased away, peace is coming. At long last.

12th April 2018

I've been told to make a determined effort to finish this book and start a new one, there are people passing over all the time… but first there have been other books to write and second, even now very few C&W artists have come to visit, so this section will be quite small.

Mr John says:

Not sure why the artists aren't pouring in, perhaps they will for the second book, there'll have to be one, girl, no chance of not doing it over again. This one's taken an age to collate, got to say and I've not helped, have I? But when I got home, there was so much chattering to do, so much catching up to do and so much getting used to being a spirit to do I clean forgot about this and just enjoyed myself.

My life wasn't all roses, if it had been, I wouldn't have been the Man In Black, I would have been able to break out into colour now and then, like my friend Elvis did, rhinestones and all, although they wouldn't have suited me, would they? There were stubborn people to fight with, stubborn proud people to fight for, songs to create, music to make and people to work with, like us being the Highwaymen. That was tough going sometimes but so much fun other times, when it all came together and we got what we wanted, the right sound from the four of us.

Got to say, though, looking back over the years, they were on the whole pretty good, and what wasn't good was absorbed into the experiences of being a high profile fighter for the rights of the Native Americans. I don't want, right here, to go into the drugs and more drugs, that was an intensely personal battle which I eventually won but I think the cost was too high. I do want to say how much I loved the women in my life, especially my June. I couldn't live without her; it all fell apart when she left me for Heaven. That was something I couldn't handle.

The one thing I know is, I won't be forgotten. Controversial life, controversial songs, controversial concerts in prisons, all built my reputation and then I had to live up to it, didn't I?

Thanks for having a country section, thanks for waiting for me and the others. Some of them might opt out, others will be along to talk to you, they've promised. I'll do my best to get them here for you. Thanks for listening more than anything.

This is the Man In Black signing off.

Before The Next Teardrop Falls

Freddie Fender

June 4, 1937 – October 14, 2006

November 2008

A CD of country music is being played over and over in the car when Terry and I go to lunch and this song comes around many times. Then it began to come around when no CD had been played. Freddie is a most welcome addition to Country Roads, a gentle voice, a gentle song and a man of great feeling.

April 2018

It's been a long time… but Freddie is here tonight, possibly my last visitor of the evening. It's been busy…

Freddie says:

There were many times when I needed to stop, look in the mirror and go 'hey, Freddie, you made it but it's gonna take some work to keep you there!' It was my way of keeping my feet on the ground, because once the hits started, it became all too easy to forget I was representing the Mexican Americans in our great country who wanted to make it, too. Too easy to think it would last forever, that I was immortal. I think because of that I worked harder than the average C&W singer to make it and stay having made it; I never took fame for granted. Got to say, though, it was really good fun. Singing in English, singing in Spanish, crossing the two and joining them up, making me different, was fun. I enjoyed all of it, even as I kept an eye on the ground and made sure both feet were standing on it at all times. I had no real illusions but can tell you now I was so grateful it carried on, that the awards were there, the recognition was there as it paved the way for others. I quite liked being a trailbreaker for other Mexican Americans.

Not much else to say really, I do help those who are striving to break down prejudice and become stars in their own right, and they will! I've seen such talent and that talent I help where and when I can. Like others in this book, I want to make the most of what I can do from the spirit world.

Thanks for waiting for me, thanks for listening to me. Best of luck, chica.

Sixteen Tons

Tennessee Ernie Ford

February 13, 1919 – October 17, 1991

I've had Ernie Ford's name in this book for what feels like an age, possibly ten years, as most of the C&W stars called their name at the same time and then nothing happened... too busy having a good time, it seems! But today, 1st May 2018, both Ernie Ford and Faron Young visited to say they would be back and they are.

Ernie says:

Not planning to go on very long, friends and fans, just to say I had a wonderful time, either singing the country stuff or the gospel and don't go asking me which one I liked the best, they both meant everything to me. Fame sat easy on me as if I always knew I would make it. Radio, records, TV, all were easy to conquer and I felt at home with it all. So, you can ask and I can't answer, why the drinking? I think drink is as potent a problem as any drug, it gets you, it won't let go. But – got to say this too, I enjoyed the drinking, where I don't think I would have enjoyed drugs.

That takes me away a little from why I'm here, which is to say thanks to all who gave me a hand to get into each branch where I became a star, you're all great people. And to all who bought the records, liked the music, liked the singing and all, thanks!

So there I am, immortalised in your book, dear channel. Sorry about the wait... like you said, having too good a time...

King Of The Road

Roger Miller

January 2, 1936 – October 25, 1992

'Little Green Apples' has been given to me several times, one of Roger's hits, but not the one he wanted to headline his chapter, of course, that had to be his greatest hit of all. It is September 2008 and I am happy to welcome Roger Miller to Country Roads.

It's May 2018 – time to wrap this up as soon as I can; more books to write… but not without filling as many empty pages as I can. Roger Miller's here tonight –

Roger says:

Bad beginning, sad ending, in between a lot of songs, a lot of singing, a lot of friends and a world of love. I think that's pretty much the way it was and still is, I know there's a whole load of people who remember me with love. Trust me on this one if you will, the love you carry for those who pass over carries right on reaching them.

The honky-tonk novelty songs did well for me, and did I ever love writing and singing them, too. Writing them myself meant I phrased everything to suit my voice, rather than massacre someone else's, though I did that too. King of the Road is one of my favourites, not only because it was the huge, huge hit I never dreamed it would be but because it all fell into place so easy when I was writing it. I smiled all the way through.

Thanks for the support and appreciation, all you fans, thanks for being there, family and friends. Cancer's not good but better than some other ways of going. I've no complaints.

Behind Closed Doors

Charlie Rich

14th December 1932 – 25th July 1995

September 2008
No sooner had Country Roads been proposed than I got
'The Most Beautiful Girl' given to me and knew Charlie
Rich was around. He is most welcome to Country
Roads. He decided to have Behind Closed Doors as his
chapter heading, saying it is his favourite of all that he
sang.

October, 2008:
I am pleased to say the Silver Fox has been around on
and off, singing that song and making me smile by his
very presence, a sense of sunshine and lightness
guaranteed to lift anyone's spirits. This is one lovely
man.

Charlie says:

As this channel has just discovered from a brief
overview of my career, it was pretty much hit and miss,
with more miss than hit most of the time. Somehow the
music never quite gelled with people because I played
across the whole spectrum, I went from jazz through
blues to country and it never really connected much
anywhere until the record company pushed me into the
C&W field and then it settled down a bit. But, all that
uncertainty and bitter disappointment drove me to drink.
All right, that's an excuse, others have had worse times
and not drunk, but then again still others had worse times
and went to drugs. Sometimes you can't win in an
industry that seems determined to throw you out, no

matter how good your material, no matter how hard you try. I know my channel has found this many times with her books, how she has tried and how she has been knocked back time after time. It is to her credit she never turned to drink, but that was my way out.

Singing, making music and writing songs was everything to me. I wanted to sing, wanted to make music like you would not believe, so much that it hurt. And that hurt shows. We just looked at the home page of my official website – would you believe I have such a thing? – and there I am, all sad eyes and loneliness. That about sums it up, to be truthful. It wasn't an easy life and it wasn't a good life but I lived it and I appreciated being able to live it. Even with its bad times, I doubt I would have been any happier doing anything else.

So, what am I doing now? That seems to be the question everyone gets asked, so I am answering it before the channel asks, save her the job. I work with those who are being knocked back by the record companies and the record buying public. I try and bolster them, give them the strength to try another door, another song, another demo to another company. Sometimes you get through. It's harder work than living it, in some ways, but rewarding, because a couple of them actually made it.

That made it all worthwhile.

Thanks, dear one, for this chance. It has helped a lot to know I can come to someone and talk with them, be around them and draw on the aura of happiness and laughter that seems to surround you, due in part to your great love for all spirit people and in the other part to the madness of those companions of yours. They're great; don't let anyone tell you otherwise.

I will be back, listen out for me.

Ongoing – Charlie has indeed been back, he visited today to say hi and ask how I am, making me smile by his presence as he did before.   Thank you, Charlie, you are such a lovely person!

It's 4 In The Morning

Faron Young

February 25, 1932 – December 10, 1996

October 2008

I have been given 'It's 4 In The Morning' several times, but not strongly enough to push me to look up Faron Young on the Internet. This morning the prompting was that strong and I looked, to find the great under-rated Faron Young had indeed gone home, through a self inflicted gunshot. Sadness abounds in the music industry. I am more than happy to welcome Faron to Country Roads. There is a deep sense of loneliness and sadness in his music which I appreciated before I knew how he had passed.

I am looking forward to Faron coming to speak with me, when he is ready. For the moment he tells me it is enough to be recognised and accepted.

May 2018

Today Faron told me he would be back with his message. It's only taken 10 years, he said…

Faron says:

The sad thing is, I loved to sing, loved to act too but singing came first and yet even that great love and ability which I had was not enough to fight off the depression which I fought with drink. Vicious circle which I know a lot of 'famous people' have become trapped in over the years. I've seen it myself and knew it

161

might be my end, without really appreciating that it would be. I should have fought harder to escape but really, sometimes it's easier to give in. The greater sadness is not seeing my children get on with their lives from your side of being, rather than from here.

The accolades were good, were comforting, were encouraging but again, not quite enough to lift me from the depression that haunted me like a huge black cloud that never let the sunshine through.

I don't want this to be a depressing message; it's me telling you the truth. I am so grateful to all who bought the records, saw the films, were faithful fans to the end. I haven't lost sight of all that I meant to people or what you all meant to me. Thank you from my heart. Just know that coming to this side of life meant leaving that huge black cloud behind. I couldn't have gone on any longer.

Your Cheatin' Heart

Hank Williams

September 17, 1923 – January 1, 1953

December 2008

Your Cheatin' Heart kept coming into my head over and over, as these 'I am here' songs do and I recognised and greeted Hank Williams with great pleasure this morning. I'm hoping he'll come soon to talk to me about a great career and songs which have endured.

May 2018

Hank says:

Your hope I'd come soon and talk didn't work out, did it, sorry about that! Here I am, 10 years down the line, coming to talk at last. Not got a lot to say but I sure want to be in this book, hell, I'm in everything else, all those artists who covered my songs, all the people who wanted to sing and play like me and went right ahead and learned to do it, in all those 'halls of fame' and mentioned in high places in the music world – not bad for someone who only managed 29 years, what do you think?

Trouble is, damn drink, damn drugs, damn body that didn't hold up to the abuse I gave it. Others went on and on with the same problems as me, how come I had to go give way? 'One of those things' they told me when I got over here. Still, it's nice not being ill, not being dependent on anything, being able to work with those who still want to sing the Hank Williams way. Just be sure to let them know prescription drugs and drink don't mix.

Take Me Home, Country Roads

John Denver

December 31, 1943 – October 12, 1997

Sometimes books surprise me, sometimes people surprise me. This book has been a combination of both. I mentioned to the publisher that I needed to work on the C&W section. He emailed back he'd send out a call for John Denver to come to me.

He did, I had a vision the very next day (22nd April 2018) of John sitting on the wing of the plane waving to me...

John says:

There's a quite a lot of us gone over through aircraft accidents. I realised that when I saw the pages flipping by as the channel searched for my page. I have to think, well, it was over pretty quick, I had 54 years of good life, no cancer or lung conditions or disability that cripple and make each day a living torment. Only the drink.

    Problem is; my death would have been avoidable if the switches had been better positioned. I recall reaching wildly for the switch, recall seeing the fuel disappearing at an alarming rate and knowing, just knowing, it wasn't going to happen, I'd no chance of accessing the tank, no way of refuelling, no way of escaping a death which was foolish and at that point, unavoidable. If that lot sounds complicated, it's still tough even now to think about it; wasn't my body which let me down but the design of the plane. But there's no point in dwelling on it, what happened, happened and I ended up here and I love it.

I mean, how many songs did I write and record? Were there any more to be found in the muddled addled brain I had by then? (Drink does that) Flying was wonderful, I felt a great sense of release and contentment when out there in a plane, so it was all designed to be, end of life in a plane I designed and – up to that moment – loved and thought there was a future for it.

Want to say thanks here to the millions of fans who bought the music, to the recording people who made them so good, you know who you are, to Stuart who called me to come – I'd missed out on this book, not sure how – and thanks to the channel for her patience in transcribing this tonight. Not the easiest of messages, even after this length of time it bugs me that I died in such a stupid and wasteful accident. That was an expensive piece of flying equipment…

SECTION 3 – COLOUR ME BLUES

With the help of Alexis Korner

Long John Baldry – *Let The Heartaches Begin*
Big Bill Broonsy, *I Believe I'll Go Back Home*
Arthur 'Big Boy' Crudup, *That's All Right Mama*
Reverend Gary Davis, *Twelve Gates To The City*
Sleepy John Estes, *Worried Life Blues*
Blind Boy Fuller, *Big House Bound*
John Lee Hooker, *Dimples*
Son House, *Death Letter Blues*
Elmore James, *Dust My Broom*
Blind Lemon Jefferson, *Long Lonesome Blues*
Robert Johnson, *Cross Road Blues*
Alexis Korner, *Whole Lotta Love*
Lead Belly, *Where Did You Sleep Last Night?*
Bessie Smith, *Downhearted Blues*
Sonny Terry and Brownie McGhee, *Key To the Highway*
Stevie Ray Vaughan –*Texas Flood*
Muddy Waters, *Got My Mojo Working*
Gary Moore, *Still Got The Blues For You*
Howlin' Wolf, *Smokestack Lightning*

Introduction

This section came as a surprise and yet on reflection, maybe it was not so much of a surprise. The pop artists section was going well when the blues men decided they wanted recognition too. Fortunately, after a relatively long marriage to someone with a lifelong love of the blues, the names are extremely familiar to me, along with their music. I asked for a title and was given Colour Me Blues: when I asked who had thought of it, I was told John Lee Hooker. I say thank you to John; it's superb!

In September 2008 that great modern blues man Alexis Korner shouted his name to me and volunteered to be the person to bring the old musicians and singers to me for the book. I was and am thrilled and honoured to have Alexis working with me on Colour Me Blues.

The blues men cover many years and many songs; blues have a long tradition of putting sorrows and burdens to music, to sing out the sadness and in doing so, bringing pleasure to many, many people. This section is a chance for the blues men to show how they were influenced by their music, to talk of their time in the Realms and their work either there or here, and for us to remember them. Most of all, it is for us to remember them, for their great music should not be forgotten.

Let The Heartaches Begin

Long John Baldry

12 January 1941 – 21 July 2005

Long John's name has been here for a long, long time, now I'm working to finish this book once and for all, people are arriving, prodded, I do believe, by John Lee Hooker, who's busy rounding them up for me.

May 2018

Long John says:

My name's been here for a long time, that's right! Been enjoying my new life so much I clean forgot how time passes on your side of life.

It was good, but then we all say that when fame's river is flowing our way, when our music is wanted, when the audiences are there, we say it was good. Some of us got the chance to go on making it good. Me, I went down with that accursed chest infection which ended my time with you. But then… I wonder if it could have gone on much longer, things were troublesome, personal life, mental strife, friends with mental and personal strife I was working with, and magical wonderful friends like Rod Stewart who worked with me. It was a circle of caring and if I had to suffer it all over again, I would for the sake of knowing true caring people are out there.

I loved to sing, still do. We have times here when us singers get together and relive some of our favourite (not best, favourite) songs and remember with each other how it was. Then we say 'well, it was good while it lasted' and go back to what we were doing – helping those of you on your side of life who want to sing, who want to play, who want to come out and haven't got the nerve – do it! Nothing worse than concealing what and who you are.

Be strong, people. It seems to me your world is getting harder by the year. You can rely on those of us who are reaching out to you to give you a hand. Don't ignore it, we all need help. I know I did and there's no end yet to the thanks I am giving Rod for all he did for me.

Go see what you can do for someone, right?

I Believe I'll Go Back Home

Big Bill Broonsy

June 26, 1903– August 14, 1958

October 2008

and the Big Man himself is here, laughing over my trying to track down his name, which I was mis-spelling! He didn't tell me, of course... he let me find out for myself. Much laughter going on here, I can sense it and feel it. It took a while for Big Bill to decide which song he wanted as his chapter heading but finally settled on this one, which he says meant a lot to him. I am more than glad to welcome Big Bill to Colour Me Blues, a man of his stature could not be left out.

May 2018

Working to close this book, to fill the empty pages where there is just a name, this evening I am calling on Big Bill to come and talk to me about his varied, comprehensive career, one which survived against all the odds. And to straighten out the dates, I had a real mixture on this page for the longest time.

Big Bill says:

What's so important about a few dates then? What you got there is good enough, near enough my shortened life. Damn cancer holds no liking for any of us folks, whether we be done living or not. I'm just glad I got to sing me a lot of songs and get them on records for others to listen to, so I know it ain't gonna get lost in the mists of time. My heart and soul's in them records.

Mind you, when I got started I never thought it'd go that far, that someone would want to record me. I just wanted to do the singing to the folks who knew what the songs meant and how much of me was in each and every one of them. Good times, very good times, even when the records didn't sell too well and I had to go on working. I didn't mind work, good for the body, good for the mind and something to do all day long, too. Always the evenings to play the guitar and sing the songs.

Thanks to the world for accepting and remembering Big Bill. Does warm my heart so to see how many big names in the singing world cite me as inspiration. Magic, so it is.

That's All Right Mama

Arthur 'Big Boy' Crudup

24th August 1905 — 28th March 1974

October 2008

Reading about Elvis Presley obviously bought Arthur Crudup's name to my attention. I didn't wait for Alexis to bring him; I asked if he wished to be included. I experienced a long pause and then heard 'I might and then again I might not.' This was followed by a booming infectious laugh and then I heard 'of course I want to be in there!' So Arthur 'Big Boy' Crudup is included. I wait on his coming to see me to talk about his life and music.

It's May 2018 and my determination to try and close this book has brought the 'missing' people to my home. Arthur Crudup is one of them.

Arthur says:

From gospel to the rocker man doing my songs, my work's out there and that's all I need to know to let me be content. It weren't easy at that time, got robbed of royalties, got robbed of time and peace of mind often enough too, but the blues was there for me and they saw me through it. Some good times, some rare good times singing with the greats, then like I said, seeing my songs going on into your time. Magic! Got to say it's a good feeling and I can rest easy on that.

    Thanks to everyone who worked with me and for me to get the money I was due, the recording people, the others who were there doing their part in making my life that bit better. I got lucky, there's many far worse off than me.

Thanks for waiting!

Twelve Gates To The City

Reverend Gary Davis

April 30, 1896 – May 5, 1972

October 2008

The Reverend Gary Davis is with me. He was also known as Blind Gary Davis, but the Reverend part is extremely important to him still, his conversion to Christianity and his becoming a Baptist minister were and are an essential part of what makes this blues man so special.

The Reverend says:

I am surprised and pleased to see so much information is out there on my life, that website, strange thing that it is, dedicated to me and such kind comments from others who have learned from my guitar playing. I want to thank every one of the people who have worked on these things, have put my music together in that way for others to learn from, to play, to appreciate, to be happy listening to the songs.

I had difficulty finding the one song that means the most to me, to be the chapter heading here for my page. But Twelve Gates To The City is a fine song, says a lot about the way I saw heaven then, thought of it as a city, where it is in truth a Realm, a vast endless place of great beauty, great love, great understanding. But the song stands as a testament to my belief at the time; I have good memories of it.

Seems like many who come to you, dear channel, say they enjoyed their life. Well, it's true of me too. I had a good time making music, making records, I had a better time when I found the Lord and became a minister and could help save souls and advise others on the great love that the Lord Jesus brought to us all. I loved my gospel and spiritual songs as much as I loved my blues songs. The Lord knows I did my best with what He gave me, a voice, an ability to play guitar, and an audience for the songs and the music. I am so grateful to Him for all I had in life and for what I have now.

I don't want to dwell much on it all, just to say thank you to you all and thank you to this dear one for letting me come and speak with her. She is a good channel, she knows our presence without us having to say who we are. It is a fine book to write, a good thing to put together. Us old bluesmen need our recognition!

Thanks be to God I am still alive and well and able to sing my songs. If any new blues people out there think they have a presence around them sometimes, saying 'play it like this and sing it like that' and think they recognise it from one of my records, then they sure enough will be speaking with me. It's the least I can do.

Big House Bound

Blind Boy Fuller

July 10, 1907[1] - February 13, 1941

Blind Boy's name came to me along with Big Bill
Broonsy in early October 2008. I know his photograph
well from the LP we had at home. He is welcome to the
pages of Colour Me Blues, another influential name
from the world of blues.

May 2018

Blind Boy Fuller's name has been here for over ten
years, he's linked with many of the greats, he's a giant
amongst the old blues men. I have been waiting for him
to come. Brownie McGhee was here a few minutes ago,
these two men are linked and I wondered if Blind Boy
would come. He said 'I'm here!' just when I thought I
would have to close the page. He's saying 'call me
Fuller,' so I am.

Fuller says:

None of us can say our lives were easy, always
something to go wrong somewhere along the days. Like
my losing my sight. When you've seen colour and
beauty, when you've looked on faces you love, it's very
hard to walk into that darkness and accept it. In a lot of
ways, it benefited me as I turned to something else other
than my usual job, which I couldn't do any more and so I
ended up singing the blues music and getting to know
some of the other blues musicians and making the most
of what could have been a disaster. With the Lord's help
we can turn just about anything round. It's true I had a

terrible temper, couldn't control it and it ruined a few chances for me but not as many as Old Man Death coming calling when I was not that old. Wished I'd had more time but then – thinking about it – don't we all say that when our time's done?

You're gonna ask, what are you doing now from the Realms? I'm working with people who lose their sight. It's much harder than being born blind, then you never know what you're missing. I do my best…

Worried Life Blues

Sleepy John Estes

25 January 1899 or 1904[2] — 5 June 1977

Sleepy John Estes is one of the big names in the blues world and what a great blues name to have!

I know John's music from the many blues programmes I listened to over the years, he has a distinctive voice and distinctive lyrics, too.

Sleepy John says:

If ever there was a good music form, blues is it. You can do whatever you want, sing it how you want, play it how you want, like boogie, like field hollers, like low down draggy songs that tear your heart out and give it you on a plate, there ain't nothing like blues. Never has been, never will be. Them's as takes the music and makes it electric, well, they're bringing it to a new generation. This channel doesn't know yet but she's about to find out – she went to a gig when the Blues Band, that modern sensation, were touring and celebrating 25 years of playing together and making that good blues music. I was there with her. That was some night! She talks of it still to any who will listen for that was right fine music, starting off slow and acoustic and then rocking and boogieing and bringing the place down.

But I go back, back to the old 'uns, them as started this blues thing going. I done sung my songs and played my music and heard the audience shout it back at me and that were good, real good. It were an up and down life, I have to say, it got me out of the fields and into the studio but then it all sort of went and I was down on my luck for years and then it all sort of came back again, like a big circle turning itself around. It gave me a chance to perform and I took it and it was good.

Can I say I would not have changed much of that life, no matter how I look back on it being a bit up and down, and how I could have done without being quite so poor but still – it gives you a new look at what you have and what you need in your life. Faith in yourself most of all, hang on to that, believe you are a good person, and it comes right. Sure enough does come right.

What am I doing in the realms these days? Helping those who are hard up, in poverty. I found ways to live and I show others the way, where to get food, where to get help, where to get shelter when they need it. I work with the homeless and the hard up and they sometimes – just sometimes – know someone helped and say thank you but mostly they look on it as luck and that's all right by me. I done my bit and that's all that matters.

Thank you, dear channel, what a gift this is, what a chance this is for us old 'uns to speak on our life and our music and be immortalised forever in words!

Dimples

John Lee Hooker

August 22, 1917 – June 21, 2001

September 2008: It is good to record that John Lee Hooker was the first of the blues men to come and visit, to record his feelings and thoughts for the book, as the title is credited to him. He took some time to decide which of his hits would be the heading for his page, but finally he settled on Dimples and seems glad he did so.

John Lee Hooker was highly influential in the blues world, crossing over into the boogie-woogie style of music too. His style was a half-talking, half-singing way of expressing himself which made him different from the others. He was charismatic and prolific; his discography just goes on and on and on...

John says:

Early life was not happy, although I had a good grounding in spiritual songs and music before I was old enough to know any different. My stepfather taught me guitar but I have to say I was not unhappy to lit out of there and go travelling, working where I could, singing where I could. My fame in the music world rather took me by surprise at first, but then it was good, very good, with money from the recordings, so many of them! But then I didn't need days and days to lay down the tracks; I got in the studio, sang my songs, played my guitar, and got the hell out again. No problem to me. How some of these groups take weeks, months even to do an album is still beyond me. Get in there, give your heart to the music, get out, get writing the next one. Where's the trouble and problem in that?

I was a happy blues man when the recordings took off, when I found people wanted to hear me, paid to hear me! Man, that was something else. So many of the old guys died in virtual poverty compared with what I had and I know it and I appreciate it and I have done my best from this side of life to give a little of it back. If I find anyone playing blues guitar, putting them blues words down, I am there, dropping hints, touching the strings, sorting it out as best I can, giving them the urge to carry on. The blues is everything, man, I do tell you that. Blues hits us all in the heart, stomach and guts, we all get our troubles, we all have to sing the sad songs. Blues does it better than just about anything else.

I'm right glad to be mentioned in this book, dear one, thank you. I am right glad you like my title so much, I done dreamed it up one night when I thought about the other book you were busy writing and I thought, hell, us blues men need our own voice, our own recognition, our own memorial, our own immortality. Yes, I done read the words you chose and I done think they're great.

To everyone who bought my stuff, who still buy my stuff, who play my music on the radio, who mention me from time to time, thank you. I played for you all with my heart, with my soul, with all I had to offer. I thank you for accepting it and accepting me.

I thank you too, dear one, for allowing me to come close and for writing my words. It's been a pleasure to be with you.

Death Letter Blues

Son House

1902-1988

September 2008.
The name of Son House was given to me, one of the 'heavyweight' blues men, influential, as they all were in different ways, and someone I am honoured to welcome to the pages of Colour Me Blues.

May 2018

I've been getting this book in shape and stopped at Son House's page several times. Tonight his name is being called over and over, so now I can fill this page. I am delighted to have him here.

Son says:

I thought of myself as a picker, nothing much more than that, the guitar just there to help the songs along, but looking at all the wonderful things written about me has made me see it different now. Lord, lord, if they had said that at the time I doubt I could have kept myself the way I did. I don't like them as get big headed and egoistic over their singing and playing. That's not the way it should be, we play and sing the blues because it's our heart and soul we're bringing you,

Now I'm here all the words I had in my head to say have gone, like seeds on the wind. No matter, you know who I am, I know I was honoured and humbled by the reception I got everywhere I went in later life, featured at big concerts and all. I want to thank everyone and say again, Lord, lord, thanks for being good to me.

Dust My Broom

Elmore James

27ᵗʰ January 1918 – 24ᵗʰ May 1963

October 2008

Very aware that Elmore James is making himself known and when I went to the Internet to check out his songs, *Dust My Broom* all but leapt from the screen. A classic blues song covered by many different artists, but as always, original is best. King of the Slide, Elmore James, is more than welcome to the pages of Colour Me Blues.

May 2018

And very aware Elmore James is here tonight – another page being filled with a message from another outstanding blues man.

Elmore says:

Seems hard to accept it was ten years back I called out to you I wanted to be in your book, but there it is in black and white, well, on your screen anyway. Sorry about that! Been having too good a time over here.

I don't want to dwell on the life, which was good, it really was, loved the singing, the playing, the song writing, the friendships, want to tell you how it goes down with the new blues men you've got coming along. There's a few of them got the heart and soul of the blues and it's them we're targeting. There's a bunch of us keeping an eye on the new ones coming through, we take it in turns to drop by, to whisper a hint of this change or that, this twist on the lyrics or that. It worked for the ones already come over to us, it'll work for the ones coming along now. Listen out for it on the records of new bands, ones that work tight together, ones that have the feel for the way we used to do things and bringing it to new audiences who don't know about us. That don't matter none, what matters is the blues are still alive and kicking.

Thanks for letting me go on about it.

Long Lonesome Blues

Blind Lemon Jefferson

September 24, 1893[1] or October 26, 1894[2]
or July 1897[3] – December 1929

October 2008;
It will be good to ask Blind Lemon what his actual dates
are when he comes to speak with me!

May 2018
And my working to fill this book has brought Jefferson
to me; he says 'just call me Jefferson. I never did like
being Lemon.'

Jefferson says:

Right pleased I am to read about my grave and the
cemetery, after all, no man cares to be in an unmarked
lonely grave in some unmarked lonely cemetery, do
they? The wonders of playing music that the people
liked enough to record, even paid me a bit now and then
for it, and it endures right to now, with the blues lovers
out there still remembering us old ones and the music we
made.

I was born blind; the world was one of noises which
I learned to use to find my way around. In a time when
us people weren't taken care of and in a time when blind
people were pitied but not helped, noise recognition
became very important so I never got myself hurt by
horses or animals or vehicles but I did become very
aware of music and a need in me to make good music to
tell people about life. That should be Life, I guess. So
being blind pushed me in that direction. Good things
come out of bad things, don't they?

So, overall, not a bad life but hell, was it ever short! I really thought I'd have a lot of years to sing and play so I am very pleased I got to record my songs, or you would never have known about me.

Glad you did.

Cross Road Blues

Robert Johnson

May 8, 1911 – August 16, 1938

September 2008

The whisper going round was: Robert Johnson is here. And indeed he is; the uncrowned king of the blues singers has arrived to talk to me. He comes as a gaunt, lined man, although only 27 at his passing, he appears much older in body and mind. His soul, he says, is tired and wants to find peace but he wishes to make one last statement on his music, his alleged pact with the Devil and his death before he seeks a rest from all that troubles him still.

Robert says:

I told people the story of the pact with the Devil because they did not think a black man could learn to play the guitar and sing like I did, any songs, any music, any style. Some of it I did not care for but if it earned me money then I played it and I took the money so I could eat and I could drink. Damn me if I didn't need that drink if I were to keep playing that music!

People bought the story because they liked to believe the Devil had something to do with my skills. But I tell you they were hard won through hours and hours of playing because it was something I wanted to do more than anything, more than even thinking of saving my soul. I wanted to play and sing and I did.

I lived all over the place, lived here and there and married those who were silly enough to marry me and took the women I fancied because they fancied me. I was a loving man, if you get my meaning. But I had devils haunting me, devils in my mind. I drank to kill those devils but they would not stay dead, when the drink wore off they were there, taunting me again. I wrote some of them out in my songs, that Hell Hound, he done tormented me for years.

I could lose the devils for a while if I played the music; they could not get past the music.

I did so love to be with the other blues players, when we would strike those chords and bring on the singing and the bottles and we could lose ourselves in the miseries we created by being alive.

I did so love it when they recorded my songs and there were the records with my music on them, preserved forever. Sometimes you get immortality without looking for it. I found out from watching and listening to you people on your side of life that my music and my name lives on. That makes it all worthwhile.

The word seems to be that I was poisoned. I wasn't. I took ill and died from too much booze and too little decent food and quiet living. Why that story went around I don't know but it ain't true and it is time it was laid to rest.

I want to say thank you to this one for speaking with me. She is a fine channel and a good receiver of us musicians and singers. She knows our vibrations, she welcomes us and that's a damn fine thing if ever there was.

Blues fans of the world, I thank you for keeping my music alive. It was my heart and soul you got in those records, right glad am I that they are still there.

Whole Lotta Love

Alexis Korner (with his band CCS)

19th April 1928 – 1st Jan 1984

September 2008 –

Alexis Korner literally shouted his name to me in the early hours of the morning as I lay awake. I remember Alexis very well from the blues programmes we listened to, from his outstanding recordings with his band CCS and recalled the long tragic decline as Andy Kershaw sat in for him week after week, starting every programme by sending Alexis good wishes for a speedy recovery when we all knew that it was terminal. Such sadness, to lose at 55 so great a talent and driving force in the modern blues field as Alexis. (I've been listening to CCS on my car stereo, it's fine driving music!)

This September morning we discussed his being the one to bring me the blues men and this he said he would love to do. He came with such energy and vitality that it was clear he needed a project, this is it. Up to now it has been the first person to come to me who has become the shepherd, as it were, but as at this date, 14th September, although I had been given the title and people were coming, no one had volunteered the task of gathering people up and bringing them to me. It was as if they were standing back, waiting for the right person. He came this day and I am more than pleased to know he is here and ready to work. I am getting my usual confirmation YES to these statements. Alexis just said: 'they all stood back and waited for me, knowing I was coming.' Maybe they knew he had more energy than he knew what to do with, so he was 'volunteered' for the job without him realising it…

Putting this part of the book together is a great honour for me for these men – and women – are respected and venerated for their contribution to the blues scene and the music scene generally, for so many musicians today 'borrowed' from these great men and turned the music to their own style and advantage. The songs live on, too.

Quick aside, October, 2008, during the evening I paused in my typing (dictation from a spirit author) to see my keyboard covered in lights, as if someone was typing. I heard CCS in my head, so I knew it was Alexis who was around. The next morning he asked if it was all right to pick up his emails when I logged on…

May 2018

It's been a long time coming but Alexis and I have all but wrapped up Voices now. 2-3 more blues men and 1 blues lady to come... and Alexis himself has yet to give me his message for the world. I'm aware of him here now, overshadowing me, ready to speak.

Alexis says:

The cancer diagnosis is something every cancer sufferer hates with a deadly violent hatred. I am just the same, when they told me I almost went crazy. Lung cancer. One you can't always operate on very successfully.

Before then, though, a life in and with and around music. It was everything to me, breath of life, blood rushing through the veins, I mean, check out some of the incredible musicians I worked with in the various bands formed and recorded and out there in the world. I guess we had to have Whole Lotta Love for the heading, the most famous one of the lot, lucrative too, and we did

191

give our all when we recorded that, in case you hadn't realised it...

Fellow musicians, all of you who are on my side of life and those on your side of life, I loved working with you and being with you. I loved the way it all came together and produced the sounds, the noise, the impression, the vibrations I felt in my body. You were all a vital part of it and there aren't enough thanks for that. And the fans who kept us going and the producers who let me make programmes and to Andy Kershaw who, week after week, fronted my programme and kept saying 'when he comes back' and things like that. He knew and I knew and the world knew it weren't gonna happen but oh it was a nice thought. 55 years isn't long but I packed an awful lot into it, didn't I?

Thanks for working with me, dear one, thanks for this section of your message book and for realising we hadn't included me...

Where Did You Sleep Last Night?

Lead Belly

January, 1888 – December 6, 1949

October 2008

Of all the Lead Belly songs, this one had to head this chapter. His mournful evocative emotion-filled rendition of this great song is something every blues fan knows and appreciates.

May 2018

A lot of artists have waited ten years before coming with their message, I've got used to it… this morning I was aware Huddie Ledbetter was around. He is most welcome.

Huddie says:

Lots of songs, lots of sadness, lots of driving, lots of drinking and back to lots of songs. They was just spilling outa me all the time, so much I wanted to say to the world and the world heard some of it, for sure. That Alan Lomax, he helped me get the songs out there and if he made himself some money out of it, well, who's to say that's good or bad?

There's a lot of songs out there I wrote that have other people's names on them as writers, but there again, who's to say that's good or bad? I just wanted to play them instruments, make the music, get people listening to the words and see if anything changed. Some things did, the black issue didn't, and won't for a long time to come, far as I can see from this side of life.

It wasn't an easy life but I don't think I could have had a better one at that time. I did quite well where many musicians and singers didn't get the breaks. It's good I'm remembered, right pleased I am to see there's a foundation with my name to celebrate all I did, no songwriter could ask for more.

Thanks for waiting for me to come. Pleased to be in this book.

Downhearted Blues

Bessie Smith

July 9, 1892 or April 15, 1894– September 26, 1937

October 2008

I did wonder how many blues ladies would come. I am more than pleased that Bessie Smith came to give me her name. I now await her visit to learn more about this lady with the big voice.

May 2018 and Bessie is here. I heard her name earlier in the day so I knew this was The Night the big lady of blues came visiting.

Bessie says:

How did any black singer make it in that time? That's something I fall to wondering about sometimes, when I get deep in the memories of this life. I talked of the problems of us folk through the songs and every chance I got to say it. But it took more than one blues singer to put right the wrongs, not that you're there yet, but it's better than back then, I can tell you!

So, that lifetime, singing and sex and a lot more singing and a lot more sex. You want us folk to be honest, don't you? So I am. One man wasn't enough and one woman wasn't enough and the husband I thought was there forever didn't care much for either of those things. Fool man had no idea what he was missing in the way of pleasure. I needed that human companionship and comfort, if you like, to bolster me to get out there and sing for the many who couldn't say these things for their own selves. Those of us who had voices had to do the work for them, hoping they did the writing side and got the message out – we will not be downtrodden and downhearted forever. Proving it now, aren't we?

Singing and sex. Nothing like it. Try it... and thanks for listening to me. It was good, it could have been better but I ain't complaining.

Still Got The Blues For You

Gary Moore

4 April 1952 – 6 February 2011

June 2011

Gary has been calling to me, over and above Elvis' gospel songs and Four Tops... there is no way I could mistake that call!

October 2011

And at last Gary has come to talk to me. Heavy blues, brilliant guitar playing, powerful onstage presence, Gary Moore is sadly, sadly missed.

Gary says:

Well, I can't say I'm enamoured of the photograph on my page on Wikipedia, but there you go, can't control everything, can I? Wish I could... then my air brushed picture would be everywhere...

Life, good. Music, amazing. Thin Lizzie, Skid Row; magnificent people to work with. We knew how to rock the blues, didn't we? Working with BB King and George Harrison, I mean, no words, man, no words. But the solo work was the true love, the ability to really do my own thing, produce my own music, go into a five minute guitar break on Still Got The Blues if I wanted to.

It was over too soon. I didn't know I had a bad heart, well, not to that extent anyway. We all know the old pump is gonna stop working one day, it's just that mine stopped earlier than I thought, hoped or dreamed it would.

But –look at all the accolades and compliments and memories that came out! Look how everyone reacted. Almost made it worthwhile dying, that it did! And then you were there, waiting, and I knew I had to call to you for this book. One day someone will turn to this book and say 'Gary Moore? I remember him – I think.' I know you will, you had all the music and you loved all the music and you said once: 'I wish I could see Gary playing live' and I went and died and deprived you of the chance. So here I am, in person/spirit instead. I hope this compensates... it's not the same as sitting in the audience when I'm giving it my all, but you're getting all of me at this moment. The smile says it's enough.

Thanks to everyone for making it one hell of a ride. The crash was unavoidable, sorry to say. Thanks for writing this for me. Thanks for letting me be part of this book. My love to you.

Texas Flood

Stevie Ray Vaughan

October 3, 1954– August 27, 1990

May 2018

Stevie Ray Vaughan is here to talk to me. He's no
stranger to my life; he often calls in to talk when I play
the heavy blues/rock music that really reaches me. It's
the music he loved to play.

Stevie Ray says:

If ever something ended too soon, it was my life. Oh I
had music and more music to play, as much for me as
the audience and oh how the audiences loved the music.
But the damned (excuse me) pilot done flew too low and
crashed us into the mountain and we were all dead
before we could conceive what had happened to us. I
know this because we were stood around like dumb
creatures staring at the wreckage of the heli and our
bodies and saying things like: 'what the hell happened
there?' and other polite ways of saying WTF went
wrong?'

Then we all sort of found the pathway to the realms
and stood around a bit more, consoling each other that at
least it was quick and we weren't ill or had cancer or
anything like that, we were there, we were not there. We
were someplace else and the life we had was gone, done,
dusted; finished.

Sorry? Yes, for the longest time I was sorry, angry,
bitter it had been cut off like that. Oh it did mean I left
behind the drugs, drink and aggro of being on the road,
believe me there is so much aggro in being on the road,

but the music, the audience interaction, the sheer joy of the guitar in my hands and the sounds coming alive in the auditorium and the drummer behind me matching every note and the others on stage with me and I can get teared up even now just thinking about it. I mean, I was only 35. Could have had same again, or perhaps them drugs would have got me before then or the drink, oh I needed the drink...

Now it's OK, accepted, learned lessons from that life and will take them into the next one, when I get myself together here to choose another life. I want to go on, I want to live again at least once more, learn some more lessons. Very aware this soul needs more tuition to handle the things Life throws at you. In the meantime, I am thrilled and humbled by the figures I just saw on the screen, over 5 million people had watched my Voodoo Child performance. I doubt I could have reached that many in my lifetime, but then this magical Internet brings everything and everyone into all homes, if they want it to, and I'm still there, performing, bringing pleasure to people who want to hear the songs. I guess it could have been a lot worse, the fingers could have seized up with all that movement and then I would have been impossible to live with!

Done said more than I intended but it feels good to say it. This one's a good friend, always there when I want to drop in, listen to music and talk a little talk. My thanks go there and to all of you, every last one of you who bought the music and heard the music and paid to see me play the music. Without you it wouldn't have lasted as long as it did.

Thanks.

Key To the Highway

Sonny Terry and Brownie McGhee

Sonny Terry
30 March 1914 — 1 June 1948
Brownie McGhee
November 30, 1915 - February 16, 1996

October 2008

Individually these two great blues men recorded some very fine music indeed. Together they became a partnership that worked in so many ways.

May 2018
And I know Sonny Terry is here tonight. He said Brownie will be along later, possibly not today... no problem, as long as he comes. One of my abiding blues memories is of recording a live performance of these two great singers collaborating on a song which essentially said, 'the blues had a baby and they called it rock and roll.'

Sonny says:

We talk a lot about 'what if' and here's the 'what if', if I hadn't done damaged my eyes, I'd not have played that blues harp for real, to earn money and I wouldn't have linked up with Brownie and Lord did we ever make fine music together! None of that would have happened. So, you people who play 'what if' in your own lives, remember everything's for a reason.

I had a good life. I played the music I loved with people I cared about, real friends, closer than family some of them. All because my eyes were no good to me. Didn't matter, my mouth worked well enough to sing the songs and play the harp and make the whoops and hollas the songs needed, says me anyway. We sold enough records and were paid to sing our songs enough places to know it worked. All of it worked.

Listen up, any of you reading this who've got this wrong with you or that wrong with you, it can be overcome, you think of other things you can do instead of what you planned on doing and see how well it works out. It will. It's all laid out for you, just go get it. I did, Brownie did and all them that played with us did and it was – great. Like being here, being given a chance to leave a message for all and any who remember me. Us. Brownie'll be here tomorrow. That's all from me. Thanks.

*****

Brownie McGhee arrived with laughter and the words 'look me up, look me up!' a reference to my jumping into Wikipedia each time someone comes to be sure I have their dates right and have a lightning overall look at their lives. Brownie's humour is very obvious!

Brownie says:

Didn't quite make it tomorrow as Sonny predicted but here I am, walking tall and singing loud just like I did back then when Sonny wailed that harp and we knocked those audiences out with our blues and our music. Were they ever the good days! I saw on my page it said we toured 11 months out of every year and hell yes, we did just that, collect up our few bits and pieces and travel on, travel on, as long as there was an audience waiting for us, we went. Both of us had a blues background, both of us had the blues ourselves for a hundred reasons, just like you people do now, only yours seem to be wrapped around finances and love and houses and all sorts of other things that drag you down. Gotta face up to it, we're all born with the blues and we have to just get on with it.

I have so much to be grateful for in that lifetime, getting my leg fixed so I could walk, family support, learning to play the blues music, meeting the greatest blues men ever and working with Sonny and how us two blended and played them blues! I hated the cancer that took me, it's about the only thing I wished I could have changed, found a nicer less painful way of going but I had all the rest all my life, so should I complain? I don't think so!

It's good to be here. Thanks for holding a space for me.

Got My Mojo Working

Muddy Waters

April 4, 1913, - April 30, 1983

October 2008:

An afternoon of channelling another spirit author, when I heard CCS in my head and knew Alexis had brought another bluesman to me for the book. The great Muddy Waters is here, a man revered by so many on all sides of the music field, as his work, his songs, his performances, range across the whole spectrum. His discography is long, all-embracing and diverse but it took Muddy about five seconds to choose his heading, no problem there! "This is the one," he told me.

Muddy says:

What a life! What a life, lived with music from morn to night! Singing and performing, recording and appearing on TV shows and everything, who would have thought it when I started out! It was so good, all of it, and what a pleasure it was to sing those songs and be accepted by all colours and all people. It's hard for me, sometimes, to realise how far we've come with our acceptance of colour, although there are many out there who refuse to accept us to this day. But their numbers are shrinking, slowly but surely and one day there will be no difference.

Howlin' Wolf visited this channel a few days ago and I know, because we are friends still on this other side of life like we were on that side, that he almost said the word 'black' in his communication but changed it at the last moment. I know the feeling but I will say it, we

204

were mostly black men and we were mostly not well accepted by the white folk for the longest time but the music won through in the end and we were famous for what we did, not for what we were. There's a world of difference in that.

I fought my battles, inside and outside the studio but in the end, the music was all that mattered and I got what I wanted, a solid driving beat that anyone could dance to, move to, appreciate and really come to love.

Did I have a mojo to bring me luck? Too darn right I did. It was called Love Of Music and as long as a musician has that in their heart and mind, they can't go wrong. They have to hold on to it, though, they have to live it, breathe it, sing it out to the world and let the world know what it means to them. None of this dreary stuff, this 'falling asleep over the microphone' stuff I keep hearing these days. Naming no names means making no trouble but you all know who I am talking about, there's enough of the dreary ones around, just take your pick! And then go back and listen to the real pounding music that I and others made when we were on your side of life and giving it all we had.

I want to say thank you for the chance to say this, dear one. Old Wolf told me you were a kind-hearted person, ready to listen to anyone who came, provided they came with the right heart, a good one. You know I do that, because you know my music, my name and my reputation already. Right glad I am to have visited you and met you and said these words.

What am I doing from the other side? Like many of the others, working with musicians, especially those who want to make the blues accessible to the big world. Watch out, Muddy Waters is around when you do that and influencing you, because there is nothing else but the music.

The music lives on!

Smokestack Lightning

Howlin' Wolf

June 10, 1910 – January 10, 1976

October 2008

As often happens, looking for one thing produces the name of someone else who leaps to my attention. Welcome to Colour Me Blues, Mr. Wolf... Mr Burnett. You are a name I know well and this *had* to be your song, didn't it? Above all the others, this is the one I associate most with your name and I think others probably do, too. And what is there to say about Howlin' Wolf that has not already been said by so many?

Howlin' Wolf says:

I chose me a name that would make me different from all the others and I did, didn't I? And I sang the songs that were different too, but based in the old blues,the old blues where all the heartaches and the loneliness and the drink, drugs and unfaithful women do live. Course, there is a few unfaithful men alongside of them too but us men, we don't talk about that, we prefer to sing about the unfaithful woman who leaves her man, never no mind why she had to go in the first place.

Did you hear that laughter? Your smile says you did. The old Wolf still knows how to charm, doesn't he? Yes, you're nodding at me. Yes, the old Wolf can still do it, for sure, even from this side of life!

So what of that life I had then ... you looked askance at the old Wolf when you read I walked 85 miles barefoot to find family, darn it, dear one, I did just that! But you soft living people, you ladies in your fancy shoes and boots, you couldn't do what us men did back then! Nor would we want you to. It was true and so was all the rest of it: I did make money out of my singing, my music, I did make a lot of money and I took care of them who played music and worked with me. I made money but I never lost the 'blues heart', because I knew how it felt to be poor, to have to work hard, to be rejected. I had me a damn fine woman, my lovely wife, who took good care of me and loved me with all her heart. And I loved her back the same way. If ever there was a love match, we had it. I cannot thank the Lord enough for that, not then, not now. Many men had far less than I did in my life: music, love, money, good living. I knew it. I lived it. I give thanks for it every day.

And now? What do I do from this side of life but look at you all there on that side, watch you struggling and worrying and trying to make it and right now, what is it? October, 2008, and the world is in a financial mess. Good job old Wolf ain't there right now, that's for sure. I would hate to lose my hard earned money; that I would! I've gone off the point. I don't have to worry about money but all you people still do. I want to say, go sing yourself some blues, sing your heart out, forget the money worries for a while. If any of the people there do that, and a lot do, I can tell you, old Wolf is right there, helping them sing that song. And if someone says 'my, that's a big voice' then I know I had my influence, for that is what I had, a big voice. But then you know, don't you, dear one, I was and am a big man.

This has been real fun, talking with you. I am glad to have had the chance, I seen you enough times singing your heart out in your car, singing along with the men who made up one of the great groups from the 60s and onward, those Four Tops, man, do they ever know how to sing and swing! And that white man with the black voice, that Elvis. You sure do love that man's singing, don't you, dear one? And I know well you love the man too and rightly so. He's one fine soul to have around you and how you love having him there!

Yes, I been watching you! Like the old wolf himself, I don't just walk up to someone, I slink around and watch and wait. I've been so happy watching you singing and laughing and doing the moving to the music. You love the music. That's what drew me to you, your love for the music. All of it, the blues stuff, the jazz stuff, the pop stuff, it means something to you. And the gospel, you do like the gospel, too. I heard you singing along to the gospel songs. Well, I can say you don't have a great voice but that don't matter none, you like the words, you know the meaning, you love the Lord as that great Elvis does. It's something you share and it's good.

Have you been happy to talk with the old Wolf? Yes, of course, I see the smile, the big, big smile that says yes, you've been happy to talk with the Wolf. It's been good.

You said, 'thank you for coming, it's been wonderful.' I'm saying, 'thank you for letting me come and visit, it's been wonderful.' Maybe I can drop by again some time.

Did I hear 'any time'? Thank you, dear one, I will remember that. The Wolf will return!

SECTION 4 – JAZZ INC

with the help of Fats Waller

Louis Armstrong, Hello Dolly
Josephine Baker Princess Tam Tam
Bix Biederbecke – In A Mist
Cab Calloway, Reefer Man
Duke Ellington – Satin Doll
Ray Ellington, Giddy Up A Ding Dong
Ella Fitzgerald, Oh Lady Be Good
Ted Heath – Big Band Bash
Billie Holliday, Summertime
Scott Joplin, Maple Leaf Rag
Joe Loss, Wheels Cha Cha
Humphrey Lyttleton, Bad Penny Blues
George Melly, Candy Lips
Edith Piaf, No Regrets
Harry Roy – Tiger Rag
Frank Sinatra, Fly Me To The Moon
Sarah Vaughan, Ev'ry Time We Say Goodbye
Fats Waller, Ain't Misbehavin'

Introduction

Jazz Inc came about when Fats Waller arrived and I realised he would not fit well into a book of pop singers and idols. As soon as the thought was formed, the title Jazz Inc was given to me by Fats himself. His vibrant lively rhythmic vibration never fails to make me smile.

In discussions on who would be the 'shepherd' for the people to come to me for this section, it quickly became apparent that Fats would take on this role. I am content and happy to leave the project in his capable hands. With his assistance the section cannot go wrong.

Here, then, are singers and musicians from the 'past', some will say from a time when music was more musical, when songs meant something. We have tried to cover all tastes, all styles and to bring back into the public awareness those who made major contributions to the music scene as we know it today, for their influence lives on in the legacy they left us and the foundations they created for others to build on.

Hello Dolly

Louis Armstrong

August 4, 1901 – July 6, 1971

There's no date here to say when Louis came calling but he's in the book and I'm starting at the top of the list and working my way through, to see who's around and who needs to be called at a later date... I've got used to the vagaries of the spirit authors...

Louis says:

Just been waiting my chance to drop in and say a few words to whoever's reading this book.

Good life, good career, lots of friends, lots of not such good friends but that's showbiz, you get used to it. Mostly people liked the singing and the trumpet and anything else I managed to do. Versatility ensures work, you see, especially back then when so much was emerging from the earlier music, jazz in particular.

I'm not planning on writing much, this is just a very big THANK YOU to all who enjoy the music still, I know the CDs are out there and I'm on some compilations too, especially with Wonderful World, which could have been my heading but I've long thought, if I could get into that book, it would have to be Hello Dolly, and it is!

Princesse Tam Tam

Josephine Baker

June 3, 1906 – April 12, 1975

May 2009, meditating in an effort to get the final author to come to me from those I knew were waiting but had not made themselves known, Josephine took the chance, giving me her name and that radiant smile of hers. I told her two things, 1) you are a stunningly beautiful woman and 2) welcome to my world.

April 2018

My efforts now are concentrating on getting this book finished and out to the people who we need to connect with, so the stars are remembered all over again. So I come to Josephine's page and send out a thought – are you here?

Josephine says:
I had no idea it was nine years ago I came to you! Like many others, I have been busy enjoying life in the Realms, as well as building up a whole group of singers, dancers and intellectuals who get together often to discuss world affairs. The singers and dancers just need prodding and pushing in the right direction, they'll get there and they'll be good, too. The intellectuals, the efforts they are making by simply being together and talking are making a tremendous contribution to the current world situation. I mean, do you not see the stupendous act, the crossing of frontiers in North and South Korea? That's the fruit of those working here for world peace and those on the earth who are 'working'

212

toward it in their own way, a way that sends out the right vibrations to assist us here in the Realms. It works both ways, you see.

And so... good life, even if I was denigrated for what I was back then. Now it doesn't matter, it did at that time. But for every one who disliked me for their own biased reasons, there were twenty-thirty people who did and that made the difference. I was happy enough at the time and much happier now, being here, being able to work, being able to make a contribution, a worthwhile one.

Thanks for the opportunity to talk with you. Apologies for the delay... having too much fun!

In A Mist

Bix Biederbecke

March 1903 – August 1931

It would seem that many of these jazz names were called very quickly once Jazz Inc was set up, there aren't any dates but I have had Bix Biederbecke in mind since the section was thought about. What I hadn't appreciated until then is the very short time Bix was with us and what a tremendous legacy he left us.

Bix says:

Short life, good life, did a lot, met a lot of people, made a lot of music which jazz musicians have taken and used over the years since I ended up here in the spirit world. You're asking yourself, did I regret the short life? No, I did all I wanted to do and the rest is for the other jazz men to take on into the future. Working with Louis and the other great jazz players was all the reward I wanted, the fact I made some money too was just the icing on the cake. There is always icing, it's just that others sometimes get there before you and eat it all…

But I had my share and it was good. So grateful to be remembered, so pleased to be here. Thanks for calling me back!

Reefer Man

Cab Calloway

December 25, 1907 – November 18, 1994

Singer, leader of a dance band, an example of how to dress… influential jazz player at the Cotton Club and others, Cab Calloway is one of those names and one of those people we know of without having been around at that time. His photo on Wikipedia is enough to make you smile back at him, even if you weren't around at the time he was demonstrating his great love – jazz.

Cab says:

What a life! Law studies in the day, jazz studies at night, in the end the jazz won, as it had to, thinking about it. Music is everything; music enriches your life in a hundred ways. I lived long enough and through enough changes in the music industry to see how each generation thinks they've discovered *the* music that will last forever, only to see it meld, blend and become part of something newer, something better, or simply different. Not sure if you want a lecture on musical phases but you're getting it anyway, simply because I've wanted to say this for a long time and now I've got my chance… the channel is busy and at the same time thinking 'really?' Yes, really. I wasn't just a star performer; I studied the music business from all sides and am ready to talk about it.

Music uses what's there already to move on. So, madrigals and other delightful sounds slid to one side to let the voices come through, the voices of the oppressed and the people who put their woes into words and sang them. Those blues became jazz and jazz became rock and – if you study individual songs, you will find elements of all these things right there in the mix. People respond to heavy drumming at the start of some songs, it draws them in. People also respond to a single voice with minimal background, it also draws them in. Music touches each of us somewhere, we respond to songs – they're time machines. The songs you heard at certain special times, hear them on the radio or a compilation CD, you're transported straight back to that moment. Songs and tunes, time machines. Best ones ever invented.

I've simplified the whole scene somewhat, I can't take over the book but you'll see what I want to say and understand, I hope, how the music affects you. You've no doubt gone through the list at the start of this book, the pop singers, seen names and songs that have sparked memories instantly. You've moved on to the C&W and now the jazz and the same thing is happening. 'I remember that!' is what you're thinking, or even simply feeling. My time was a long way back but you'll know of me somewhere, someone will remember and talk to you about my life in the music arena. It was good, it was great, I loved it and I am grateful I got the chance to be there, to make the music with some of the greatest names in the jazz world.

Enjoy whatever music you listen to now, dear reader, it's all good, it all resonates and gives you good, good feelings. I'm so very pleased to have had this chance to talk of my thoughts and feelings. Thanks for listening.

Satin Doll

Duke Ellington

April 29, 1899 – May 24, 1974

My early life was lived around radio rather than TV, the many radio programmes which featured music were the ones I cared about most. Duke Ellington fits into that category for me, as do Ella Fitzgerald, Sarah Vaughan and others (delighted to say they have called to me to be in this book), names most people wouldn't recognise today unless you were or are a jazz fan. I just love music – and Duke Ellington provided the world with a tremendous amount of it, written by him and performed by his orchestra. It doesn't come much better than that.

Duke says:

Music was everything to me. I felt it, sensed it, lived with it, breathed it and sent it out again in the mass of material, recorded and written, for the world to appreciate. It was a dream life, it seemed everything I did turned to something good, like going to the Cotton Club, by absorbing this musician and that one, musicians who became an integral and essential part of the orchestra. Some stayed for years, virtually their lifetimes, playing the fine music everyone loved. There are few better ways of earning a living! Live performances were always exhilarating, recordings were demanding but brought out the best in us, accolades reflected as much on the orchestra as it did on me, the composer. The awards mean a lot but the loyalty of fans means more, it is they who supported us throughout, bought the records, went to the gigs, were always there when we were there.

I'm grateful for a chance to be remembered here, too, despite all that has been done to honour me, and I am overwhelmed by the naming of parks and all in my memory, the nominations, the awards, this means a lot. It's a book that will reach a wide range of ages, and I want so much to be remembered by the young as well as the old. The music will live on forever, in this marvellous digital age you're in, nothing will escape – and I am right pleased to see that, too!

Giddy Up A Ding Dong

Ray Ellington

17 March 1916 – 28 February 1985

September 2010. The name Ray Ellington was given to me a few days ago and I smiled when I heard it. So many of my visitors have come straight from my childhood and early teen years, from listening to radio programmes where the names became so familiar they were like old friends. Ray had a wonderful career, part of which was spent working with the incredible Goons and at times it was as if he was as insane as they were. Just two days later Ray is here to talk to me.

Ray says:

The Ray Ellington Quartet was the joy of my life. Together we experimented with all kinds of music, mostly jazz with all the influences that came from the musicians who preceded us and who worked in our time. We took the music and made it our own. It was a pleasure beyond my ability to describe to you. I just loved making music.

To be involved with the Goon Show was the greatest honour any performer could have. In truth everyone connected with the show was a genius of one kind or another. The scripts were outstanding, the ad libs which went on often reduced to everyone to total hysterics, especially us who were there to provide the musical interlude, but more than that I have to say it was the synergy of those who performed. They all reacted to one another perfectly to produce comedy of a level which has never been equalled. It is my everlasting honour that I had a small part in several of the programmes quite apart from the music. I just have to ask you if you can think of anything more wonderful than making music which you love and being involved and having a part in some of the greatest comedy that has ever been recorded.

That is really all I wanted to say, just that it was a wonderful life, I could not have asked for more. I send love and thanks to all who remember me and to those who were able to give me that opportunity. I am grateful for this opportunity too, to be able to say this, and more than that, to be recognised.

I'm still making music, there are many people on this side of life would like to be entertained and I am very happy to do that. I have to repeat, I could not have asked for more.

Oh Lady Be Good

Ella Fitzgerald

April 25, 1917 – June 15, 1996

Came on a sense of laughter and happiness at being accepted.

April 2018

Ella Fitzgerald has swept in on a wave of extreme energy and laughter, obviously being in the Realms suits her well! I have so many memories of listening to Sunday radio programmes which featured her songs; it feels as if I have been hearing her name throughout my life. Some people endure where others have their moments of fame and fortune and then fade away.

Ella says:

I could have done so much more if my stupid body hadn't let me down, but that's one of the problems of being human, isn't it? Not like here, where there is no illness, no disability, no nothing to come between us and the work we want to do. What work? Like so many singers and musicians you've had come for this special book, I work with those who are talented and determined to make it in the big music world. There's a whole flood of talented youngsters coming through right now, you'll hear them soon enough. A hint here, a push there, no sense of where it's coming from, that suits me.

    Back to my life. Loved it, loved working; loved singing, loved praising the Lord, my early church days resonated with me throughout my life. I was flattered and shocked to win first prize in competitions, couldn't believe someone started a record label for my voice. But they did and I am ever grateful, even now, that I had the opportunity to do that, and to know in this time, this digital time, the music lives on in different formats but same voice, same artist, same heart.

Thanks for this chance, something else I am grateful for. Be assured all of you who bought my records, listened to my songs with appreciation, is a star in the firmament of my career. Too sentimental for words? No, you truly are stars.

East of the Sun (West of the Moon)

Ted Heath
And his orchestra

30 March 1902 – 18 November 1969

Big band music made up much of my childhood, when we really did have a wind up gramophone, in a cabinet with a hole in the side where the handle could be connected to the machine and wound up for each 78 my father wanted to play. CDs and MP3 players are light years away from that time. The music remains. No matter which bandleader's name I put into google, pages and pages come up, discography, biography, all anyone needs to know about people and their orchestras from years back. Music is a time machine on its own, isn't it? I am delighted to have the chance to talk to Ted Heath.

April 2018

Ted says:
So many big bands at that time, from Glenn Miller to mine, were all making sweet dance swing music. Call it what you will, it was and is – music. Here I admit to thinking some of your 'music' today doesn't warrant the title but then again, any music is good for the soul.

Having said that, I do hear the echo of big bands in the strings and other instruments overlaid on records by some of your major solo artists. It takes a band leader to hear it but believe me, it's there. Our influence has never gone away and never will.

I only want to say, as so many have, it was a great life, full of great influences and people. The records sold, a living was made out of something as ephemeral and important as making music.

And I just want to say the fact someone remembers me and my orchestra is all I need to keep me happy here in the realms. I am working; my hints often result in an overlay of an orchestra on those backing tracks...

Summertime

Billie Holiday

7ᵗʰ April 1915 – 17ᵗʰ July 1959

In the middle of the night, July 2008, two names came in together, two people arrived together. I had 'No Regrets' and the name Billie Holiday at the same time. Literally. Untangling this in the early hours was not easy, but I identified two visitors, Billie Holiday and Edith Piaf. Both are more than welcome to my world.

Of all Billie's recordings, she tells me *Summertime* is her favourite and so we chose that as her heading.

May 2018

This is me, making a determined effort to try and finish the jazz section of this book before I start dragging in the reluctant-but-want-to-be-remembered blues men… asking if Billie is around (getting YES…)

Billie says:

What a messed up life! If I wasn't fighting the law, I was fighting the police or the tax or the drugs or the drink or
–

But the thing which made all of this worthwhile was being able to sing. I knew I had limited range, knew some songs would be beyond me but I found the ones which worked and went with them. It was good, it got me fame and fortune and something approaching a good life from time to time.

Sorry to everyone who had ambitions for me, for those I let down through the drugs, the drink and just about everything else which came along to derail the life I had. It all got away from me, but you knew it and you supported me where and when you could. It all ended far too soon for some but not soon enough for me, my body couldn't tolerate what my mind wanted it to do/have/be. I know that now, I didn't know that then.

But oh the music goes on! The awards go on, the recognition is still there and for that I will be eternally grateful. So, the thank yous go to all who arranged for these awards to be given so the Holiday music would outlast Holiday herself. And to all who remember me. Thank you for being you.

Maple Leaf Rag

Scott Joplin

Between July 1867 and January 1868 – April 1, 1917

This was fun; I was looking for Janis Joplin's dates when I heard 'don't forget me!' and Scott Joplin slid in under the person with the same last name! Tonight, when I asked who might be visiting me to fill in a page, I thought of Scott immediately, so I knew he was around. Scott, you are most welcome to Jazz Inc, in fact it would not have been the same without you.

Scott says:

Coming as I did from a poor black background, it is a miracle that the good Lord gave me the skills to play and the imagination to create, and more than that, the people to teach me. That old teacher of mine, he worked so hard to give me a good education in music, showing me the great classical composers and how they built their music and then the operas, and of course, the piano. My first and only love. My, how I loved to send my fingers over them keys and hear the music come out in all its forms, lively, slow, blues or bright, you could make that thing do what you wanted, once you knew how.

I took myself off to go touring and playing, earning what I could where I could. As long as I was playing, I was happy.

I can't tell you to this day where the ragtime music came from, somewhere deep inside me. I was able to play out all my bad feelings in that lively music and didn't the people like it, too! Sold a few copies of the music, that we did.

I wish I could have been so happy with my women, but there you go, some things were meant to try us and losing my baby, divorcing my wife, losing my next wife ... you don't want the whole sad story of life and death and robbery and heartbreak and poverty but there it was, part of me, part of the music.

The wonderful thing is, you people still know me, still play my music and when I heard it used in that film, my, how my old heart did leap in joy! Thanks to everyone for keeping the ragtime music alive. Thanks to all who listened and bought and enjoyed when I was there with you and since I came over here, too. No need for sadness any more, I get to play as much as I want and I do help those who put their fingers on the piano keys and rejoice when the music comes out. It's a great feeling.

Thank you for all this, for the recognition, for the chance to be here. And for the good words, too!

Wheels Cha Cha

Joe Loss

22 June 1909 – 6 June 1990

April 2018

Usual process going on here… scrolling through the headed but empty pages to see which one calls me to stop, who has come with their message. Joe Loss is here!

Joe says:

I never dreamed, when I began the orchestra, that 85 years later it would still be performing! This is a dream come true, really it is.

Music was and is everything to me, to hear a full orchestra playing dance swing music is something I never got used to, never wanted to take for granted. Every performance was like the first time. Tours and concerts were the life we led, the life all of us loved, all of us who played together. I think our success came from the fact we all got on well, and Todd and Sam Watmough smoothly took over when I could no longer travel and be an essential working part of the team. It was sad for me, but I was encouraged and consoled by the fact the orchestra was still performing.

My job now? Keeping an eye on the orchestra long distance, nudging and pushing when needed. It is an ongoing thrill to know our music is still featured on radio programmes for those who love the sounds. Wonderful legacy!

Bad Penny Blues

Humphrey Lyttleton

23 May 1921 – 25 April 2008

It is the end of September 2009. I was thinking of something else entirely when Humphrey Lyttleton's name was given to me, accompanied by the sense of a huge smile and great fun and laughter. Humph had arrived, one of the major figures from the jazz and comedy scene. He was a giant figure, talented and loved by everyone. It is still hard to think of the world without him.

Humph says:

I was shocked, astonished and overwhelmingly happy when I saw the obituaries and postings which were published after my death. I honestly hadn't realised how much affection people had for me. The comments and tributes left by complete strangers were a surprise and a balm when I needed it, when I first crossed over, as there was much healing to be done to put me straight again.

What a life I had! What fun I had along the way, making music, writing, being on the radio with a bunch of extremely talented comedians and fumbling my way through what passed for chairmanship of an iconic programme – it was as if I had been given all the gifts at once and thank God I made use of them all. Not to do so would have been a waste, I think. But then I was so fortunate that everything I did gave me pleasure so at no time was any of it a chore. Family, friends, fellow musicians, fellow comics, I loved you all and I still do.

The crossing over was peaceful, after a rich and fulfilling life. Few people could ask for more and I certainly appreciated all I had and all I could give to those around me and the public, all of you out there who helped make my career what it was. Without you it would never have happened. So, thank you. I am really grateful for this chance to say this in print, thank you with all my heart for all you gave me, for being there, for listening to my music and ISIHAC too.

And thank you to this channel for accepting me without question and giving me this time. I am happy and grateful to have had the chance to meet you and work with you in this way. All blessings on the work, dear one!

Candy Lips

George Melly

17th August 1926 – 5th July 2007

George's name came to me as I idly said one morning 'are any other names going to come to me for the Jazz book?' I heard 'George Melly' immediately and had a sense of the flamboyant, outspoken, intellectual entertainer. I look forward to getting to know him better.

May 2018

Seems like I've been waiting an age for the flamboyant charismatic eccentric George to arrive, he tells me he's here, I await his words with great anticipation. And that's a fact, not just flattery, George!

George says:

What was most important to me? I had the fishing, the jazz, the art, the family, the kids, friends... I think all of it was, couldn't choose any one thing I would wish to lose out of all of it. Being President of organisations, being in front of jazz bands, being in front of an audience to talk on art – all of it mattered, all of it was a part of me. And I loved it, every moment of it. Just wish the body hadn't let me down so badly at the end, but I guess if you don't look after something, that's what happens. I could have done with an oil change and service every other year at least!

    For those who were interested in me as a person, thanks, for those who appreciated the singing, thanks, those who came to the lectures, thanks, those who shared the fishing, well, wasn't it wonderful?

Come to think of it, life was pretty wonderful. Hope yours will be, dear reader.

No Regrets

Edith Piaf

19ᵗʰ December 1915 – 10ᵗʰ October 1963

Welcome to my world, Edith.

May 2018

It is about ten years since Edith Piaf arrived along with Billie Holliday, now I am making a concentrated effort to complete the book she is here, in all her fragile beauty and delicate voice.

Edith says:

Life, whatever I was doing, was hard. The 'black dress' symbolised to me all I had lost, all I had given away, all that was taken from me. This sounds like drama and in some instances it is true that it is drama, but it was this which made the film makers recreate my life story. Through it all, through the abandonment, the many moves, the loss of so many I loved, the music resonated and kept me going. I defied anyone to stop me singing. So many came to hear me, so many loved my voice I was overwhelmed. And happy!

I chose No Regrets because now, looking back, I have no regrets. The life I had was reflected in the songs I sang and I could sing them with true emotion because I had lived them. The best comes from the heart and the tormented soul, whether it be a voice, a pen or a camera.

I am progressing as a spirit being and waiting my turn to help those who want to sing. I trust they too will have no regrets.

Tiger Rag

Harry Roy

12 January 1900 – 1 February 1971

Oh what memories! My father's favourite Big Band of all time! Harry is a most welcome visitor to Jazz Inc.

Harry says:

It was music and more music from the very early days, it was all I wanted to do, all I ever did in the end, everything else was incidental. Good records, good music, good orchestra, good friends. I didn't conquer the States as I hoped but we can't have everything. In many ways I did have everything, didn't I? and to see that my music is still being played, that there are still people who want to hear the big orchestras in full swing session is sweet to my ears.

I wish there were more orchestras working right now; I'd love to get involved in music again. Meantime I'm working with individual musicians and waiting for the world's interest in music to turn around, as it does so often, and come right back to the big orchestras again. I'll be right there, up front, loving every moment of it!

Thanks for letting me chat.

Fly Me To The Moon

Frank Sinatra

December 12, 1915 – May 14, 1998

Frank insisted that his chapter heading was Fly Me To The Moon and that he had no real reason for it, except he liked it very much.

Many smiles, sense of knowing who he was and is.

September 2008

A strange occurrence, I realised Frank was around me this afternoon (bringing me Fly Me To The Moon, not the sort of song a rock addict would have in their mind!) and a smile and a sense of companionship. Very pleasant feeling, very nice to have. I asked if he wished to come and speak and he said he did.

Frank Sinatra needs no introduction to anyone. My memories are of growing up hearing his music on the radio, on the early TV programmes, seeing him in films – he could just as easily fit into the Talking Silver book of film stars which I am building at the same time – he was and is a presence in my life. I had no difficulty in recognising his vibration either the first time or today when he came.

So, this is Frank Sinatra, Ol' Blue Eyes, multi-talented, suave, good-looking, actor, singer, man-about-town and man-with-a-mystery as many myths and legends attached themselves to him during his life and following his departure from this life, too.

Frank says:

It's a pleasure to be recognised and I thank you for that. I chose an 'unusual' song for my chapter heading, because it's one of my favourites and because you couldn't fail to recognise it when I came close and wanted to catch your attention. It worked today and it will work in the future, for I have no intention of going off and leaving you just yet! Sometimes I feel you need a bit of upliftment, another companion, someone to make you smile for a moment. Your life is not easy, I appreciate that, but it will get better, my prediction and promise to you.

Life. My life. Mixed fortunes, but overall it worked out well, didn't it? Many songs, many records, many sales, many films. What did I like doing best – acting. I loved it. Being someone else, taking on a role, stepping outside Frank Sinatra and becoming someone else. The singing was a tremendous pleasure, don't get me wrong, but the singing required no more than my voice and breath control. Acting demands much more of a person and that I was prepared to give.

The times we had, those of us in the Rat Pack, my, what times! What drinking, what orgies, what parties, what shenanigans did we get up to! Wonderful times, wonderful memories. I loved it, all of it.

Was I sad when it was over? No, not really. Everything winds down, the body winds down and when you find you can no longer do the things you used to do... in every department of life, it is time to go. I accomplished more than my three score years and ten anyway, so I was well satisfied with my life span and all that I achieved.

Now, what do I do now? Following through that first love, I work with young actors who are making their way in the profession. I guide them as best I can, urging them to the right agent, the right contact; the right connections. Sometimes it takes a push to get someone to go to a party where they will meet someone who will put them in touch with someone else and so it goes on. It is not what you know but who you know. Everyone knows this and it is one of the truest axioms of modern life. I do what I can where I can. Sometimes people aren't biddable, they resist the urging I give them and then they lose out on their chances. I can do just so much; everyone retains their freewill, after all.

Interesting life. Interesting after-life too, there is so much to do and I am more than willing to do it.

Thank you for accepting me, for listening to me, for smiling at me when I come, Dorothy. It is so good to be recognised and accepted and I realise most of us are saying that! But it is important, more than important, it pleases us and helps us realise we are still worthwhile on your side of life.

Ev'ry Time We Say Goodbye

Sarah Vaughan

March 27, 1924 – April 3, 1990

Sarah came with Ella Fitzgerald and was smiling and content.

May 2018

Sarah is here, all smiles and happiness. She is another singer from my early years; I heard her songs on the radio many times. The song she chose for her heading is one I remember well, it starts up in my head the moment I see it.

Sarah says:

What a joyous life, to be able to please people by singing! There are stories of when I was 'discovered', when I sang and played piano at this venue or that, I could spell it out but it was all so long ago it no longer matters. Facts are that I won a prize; I won a place in front of an orchestra and fulfilled all my dreams in one go. That I could go on doing it was the miracle I had never believed could happen. Wonderful life, because I loved to sing. For me singing was life and I needed to do it to continue to live.

I want to say thank you to all who helped me, all who recorded me, all who listened to me, all who made my life what it was, one long song. Thank you.

Ain't Misbehavin'

Fats Waller

21ˢᵗ May 1904 – 15ᵗʰ December 1943

It's hard to tell you what a surprise this was, listening to Roy Orbison and getting Fats Waller's name thrown at me over and over until I said 'Welcome!' Someone from my early years, heard on the radio, someone whose life crossed with mine for a few months and then he went home and I'm still here. This is someone who has a huge smile, abundant energy, masses of enthusiasm and a great love of music and people. That's my overall impression of this talented man. Among other things, he has an organisational mind, one of the first things he told me to do was look each person up in Wikipedia and print off the sheets... I didn't, because each contributor has their own ideas about what they want to say. Wikipedia is good for dates, though, so I do use it. A lot!

Fats is a great communicator, an efficient organiser, when I said I was ready to work on Jazz Inc, the singers and musicians who had already called their name were here almost immediately. It's proving to be fascinating. I'm more than grateful for his assistance, which has made this section seamlessly easy.

So here we are, 22ⁿᵈ April 2018 and Fats is ready to give me his message for you.

Fats says:

In the beginning life was a battle, not only did I lose a whole lot of siblings but my devout father didn't want me to go into music as such, he would have been happier

240

if I'd concentrated on church music but I knew, from an early age, that would not be enough for me. Once bitten by the jazz bug and, somewhere in my past, I had been bitten by the jazz bug. It's come through in the genes, there's no escaping it. Songs, piano, more songs, more piano, songs still sung today and that surprises and pleases me, for your music scene has changed so dramatically it is almost unrecognisable. That is, until you dig below the surface sounds and realise it's a bunch of people or one solo person working, playing endlessly, writing endlessly, toting it around clubs and bars and places where they can sing or play or both, ever looking for that intangible thing called 'fame' to come and find them. 99% of them don't make it but I know the same applies to so many things, writing, painting, dancing, sculpture, it all depends on that tiny extra ingredient that makes you different, outstanding, and when that happens, fame finds you.

I was lucky, I worked hard; got the exposure I needed and got the fame, too. It's a feeling you cannot describe and never really get used to, the fact others are interested in what you do so easily. Well, let's say it seems easy but it's years of work to get to that point. Just as a 'first novel' by a talented writer is invariably their 4th or 5th novel. The rest were the apprenticeship.

Like all the others, I do want to say thank you to anyone who has my records, likes my songs, remembers me with affection... you were there for me at the start and you're there for me now. I had a wonderful life overall, no complaints and being here in the Realms is just the perfect place to go on singing and writing and offering what I have to newbie songwriters, who wonder where it came from...

Finally...

This has been a joy to put together. Some names were removed, one blues man asked for his name to be removed, said he's not ready yet to come and talk, so if there is a blues section in Voices II, that's where he'll be. All those who came seemed happy with their new life, all had something to do, new roles, new work, whilst still being content to know people remember them.

My pleasure has been in talking with them, channelling their words, feeling their energy flood through me.

If this continues through all the Message books, life will be pretty wonderful!

Dorothy Davies
Servant of Spirit.

Parachute Prayer